# INSPIRING

# *Women*

*Making the most of the Christian life*

# INSPIRING

# *Women*

*Making the most of the Christian life*

CWR, Waverley Abbey House, Waverley Lane, Farnham, Surrey GU9 8EP

*National Distributors*
**UK: (and countries not listed below)**
CWR, Waverley Abbey House, Waverley Lane, Farnham, Surrey GU9 8EP.
Tel: (01252) 784700  Outside UK (44) 1252 784700
**AUSTRALIA:** CMC Australasia, PO Box 519, Belmont, Victoria 3216.  Tel: (03) 5241 3288
**CANADA:** Cook Communications Ministries, PO Box 98, 55 Woodslee Avenue, Paris, Ontario.  Tel: 1800 263 2664
**GHANA:** Challenge Enterprises of Ghana, PO Box 5723, Accra.
Tel: (021) 222437/223249  Fax: (021) 226227
**HONG KONG:** Cross Communications Ltd, 1/F, 562A Nathan Road, Kowloon.
Tel: 2780 1188  Fax: 2770 6229
**INDIA:** Crystal Communications, 10-3-18/4/1, East Marredpally, Secunderabad – 500 026.
Tel/Fax: (040) 7732801
**KENYA:** Keswick Books and Gifts Ltd, PO Box 10242, Nairobi.
Tel: (02) 331692/226047  Fax: (02) 728557
**MALAYSIA:** Salvation Book Centre (M) Sdn Bhd, 23 Jalan SS 2/64, 47300 Petaling Jaya, Selangor.  Tel: (03) 78766411/78766797  Fax: (03) 78757066/78756360
**NEW ZEALAND:** CMC Australasia, PO Box 36015, Lower Hutt.
Tel: 0800 449 408  Fax: 0800 449 049
**NIGERIA:** FBFM, Helen Baugh House, 96 St Finbarr's College Road, Akoka, Lagos.
Tel: (01) 7747429/4700218/825775/827264
**PHILIPPINES:** OMF Literature Inc, 776 Boni Avenue, Mandaluyong City.
Tel: (02) 531 2183  Fax: (02) 531 1960
**REPUBLIC OF IRELAND:** Scripture Union, 40 Talbot Street, Dublin 1. Tel: (01) 8363764
**SINGAPORE:** Armour Publishing Pte Ltd, Block 203A Henderson Road,
11–06 Henderson Industrial Park, Singapore 159546.  Tel: 6 276 9976  Fax: 6 276 7564
**SOUTH AFRICA:** Struik Christian Books, 80 MacKenzie Street, PO Box 1144,
Cape Town 8000.  Tel: (021) 462 4360  Fax: (021) 461 3612
**SRI LANKA:** Christombu Books, 27 Hospital Street, Colombo 1.  Tel: (01) 433142/328909
**TANZANIA:** CLC Christian Book Centre, PO Box 1384, Mkwepu Street, Dar es Salaam.
Tel/Fax (022) 2119439
**USA:** Cook Communications Ministries, PO Box 98, 55 Woodslee Avenue, Paris, Ontario,
Canada.  Tel: 1800 263 2664
**ZIMBABWE:** Word of Life Books, Shop 4, Memorial Building, 35 S Machel Avenue,
Harare.  Tel: (04) 781305  Fax: (04) 774739

**For email addresses, visit the CWR website: www.cwr.org.uk**
**CWR is a registered charity – number 294387**

INSPIRING WOMEN
Copyright © 2002 CWR and *Woman Alive*. Reprinted 2004

Front cover photograph: Robin Davies/Getty Images
Design and Typesetting: CWR Production and *Start*
Printed in Finland by WS Bookwell

ISBN 1-85345-223-8

Christian Life/Books for Women

Unless otherwise indicated, all Scripture references are from the Holy Bible: New International Version (NIV). Copyright © 1973, 1978, 1984 by the International Bible Society.

*Woman Alive*, Garcia Estate, Canterbury Road, Worthing, West Sussex BN13 1EH

# Contents

INTRODUCTION     Fiona Castle     1

CHAPTER ONE     Jeannette Barwick:
How to be a Secure Woman     5

CHAPTER TWO     Margaret Ellis:
Life Centre: A Dream Come True     19

CHAPTER THREE     Faith Forster:
Building a House of Prayer     31

CHAPTER FOUR     Michele Guinness:
The Binds and Blessings of Being
a Working Woman     43

CHAPTER FIVE     Liz Hansford:
Going for Growth     55

CHAPTER SIX     Reona Joly:
Everything Will Live Where
the River Goes     69

CHAPTER SEVEN     Elaine Storkey:
Twenty-first Century Freedom
for Women?     81

CHAPTER EIGHT     Liz Trundle:
Give Yourself Up     93

CHAPTER NINE     Wendy Virgo:
Your Word is a Lamp     105

CHAPTER TEN     Helena Wilkinson:
Taking Off the Mask     119

CHAPTER ELEVEN     Emmy Wilson:
A Key to Many     131

# Introduction

Many years ago, when I became a Christian, my sister Liza placed a paperback version of the *Living Bible* in my hands, together with a copy of the *Every Day with Jesus* Bible reading notes, saying, "This will help you understand what it's all about!"

Little did I realise at that moment what an impact both those publications would have on the rest of my life! The easily understandable version of the Bible, together with the notes teaching you how to apply it to daily living, were a revelation to me and provided me, a hungry new Christian, with "food for life", for which I have always been grateful.

Since that time, I have watched the author of *Every Day with Jesus*, Selwyn Hughes, expand the ministry of CWR through the acquisition and establishment of the beautiful Christian centre at Waverley Abbey House, the venue of many courses and seminars to inspire ministry and equip people to discover God's purpose for their lives. In recent years, CWR's ministry to women has encompassed the country-wide *Alive for God* tours, faith-building events for women, mounted in association with *Woman Alive*, the only British Christian magazine for women and one that helps us address a wide range of spiritual and "life" issues. I have been privileged to become involved in this work of encouraging and inspiring

Christian women, alongside powerful Bible teachers like Reona Joly and Elaine Storkey, whose ministry has challenged thousands over the years. I know they, together with other well-known speakers and writers who feature in this book, will challenge and inspire you. To mention just one of them, Emmy Wilson, co-leading a team from the church of Holy Trinity Brompton, is seeing God work in an amazing way in prisons around the country and you will be heartened to read about it in these pages.

God has a calling on the life of every one of us. Created uniquely, we are precious to Him, and our purpose, wherever we are placed, is to serve Him in our own particular way. The Christian writer Oswald Chambers expressed it memorably when he wrote: "You might as well be useful where you are, for you certainly can be of no use where you are not!"

Women have a tendency to compare themselves with others and to feel personally inadequate in the light of others' gifts and strengths. My prayer is that God may use this book to encourage and inspire you to become, uniquely, the person He wants you to be.

Fiona Castle

CHAPTER ONE

# HOW TO BE A SECURE WOMAN

*Jeannette Barwick*

# Biography

Following a career in publishing Jeannette Barwick worked as a Product Manager with an international organisation. She then led a Church community outreach project for many years. Jeannette joined the CWR team in 1984 and is now Head of Special Ministries for CWR (Crusade for World Revival), based at Waverley Christian Centre in Farnham, England.

She coordinates Selwyn Hughes' ministry in the UK and overseas, and as part of CWR's training programme teaches on temperament differences, introducing the Taylor-Johnson Temperament Analysis and the Myers-Briggs Type Indicator to several courses.

Over her many years with CWR, she has developed CWR's Ministry to Women – an aspect of the work very close to her heart. From teaching on the women's residential weekends at Waverley, this ministry takes her to cities around the UK and to many countries overseas. She finds it thrilling to see how teaching on life and relationships from a biblical perspective can be embraced by women of any culture. Jeannette has two daughters who are both married, and treasures her time with them and her four grandchildren.

Words often take their colour from their context. Take the word "love", for example. It can be used to describe the mighty passion that moves in the heart of God. The same word can be used for the affection between the sexes or the passion that some people have for chocolate brownies. One word describes several different emotions. Only the context makes clear the way the word is being used.

'Security' is a word that has to be qualified in order to understand its usage. A house or building is said to be 'secure' when it is effectively locked up and protected. A person can be said to be 'secure' when they have good financial resources. But the highest form of security I believe is *spiritual and emotional* security – the sense of inner poise that comes from knowing that one can rely on the word of a faithful and ever-loving God. That is the way I shall be using the word in this chapter.

There are a number of women in Scripture who demonstrate the kind of inner intactness that qualifies them to be described as 'secure women'. Think of Mary the mother of Jesus. How amazed and shocked this teenage girl must have been when, after being visited by the angel, she learned that she was to be the person through whom the Incarnation would take place. Notice how after that initial astonishment, she quickly recovers and says, "May it be to me as you have said" (Luke 1:38). What astonishing security and poise!

To begin to comprehend the subject of spiritual and emotional security, however, we must go back to the creation of the first human pair – Adam and Eve. The Almighty built

into them a design that was intended to be perpetuated in the rest of the human race. Part of that design was to experience, through their relationship with Him, an inner strength that would enable them to cope with any of life's demands. This inner strength is what I have in mind when I talk about "security".

Adam and Eve could be described as the world's first secure people. As long as they maintained their relationship with God, they were able to live out their lives in the knowledge that they were unconditionally loved, highly valued, and that every day had point and purpose. In a way that theologians and Bible teachers have never been able to fully understand Adam and Eve, though living in a state of absolute bliss and security, listened to the lie of Satan that they could be more fulfilled people by becoming independent of God. Though those exact words cannot be found in Scripture, that surely was the thrust of the temptation.

As a result of their wilful disobedience, every one of us born into the world since Adam has been born not with a deep inner sense of security, but with a painful longing to have our deepest needs met. Now, instead of a profound feeling of spiritual and emotional intactness at the core of our beings, we find ourselves longing to get back to what has been lost to our souls – love, value and purpose. Where once in Adam and Eve these needs were fully met in a relationship with God, now since the Fall every one of us experiences the pain of unmet needs and must learn that, though we may try other routes to meet those needs, outside of God they cannot and will never be fully met.

And here's the rub: these three things – *love, value* and *purpose* – are basic needs that simply have to be met if we are to live out our lives with a high degree of spiritual and emotional security. When we began our lives as infants, these needs were met to a certain degree by those who nurtured us. But our parents (or foster-parents), however loving and nurturing they were, were incapable of fully meeting these needs because, as I have already said, being built into us by God, they can only adequately be met by Him. Parents can begin the task of ministering to the deep spiritual and emotional needs of our personality but only God in Christ can complete it. Here's how Scripture makes the point: "For in Him dwells all the fullness of the Godhead bodily; and you are complete in Him ..." (Col. 2:9–10, NKJ). Complete in Him! Remember that. We cannot be complete in anyone else. Loved perhaps, desired perhaps, prized perhaps – but not complete.

A key issue that needs to be fixed in all our minds is: if we do not allow God to minister to our basic needs, then to the degree they remain unmet we will experience painful feelings of insecurity, inferiority and insignificance.

One of the great tragedies of life is that because of the commitment to independence that resides within us – a legacy from Adam and Eve – we tend to look in places other than God for our needs to be met. The alternative routes down which we go in an effort to find security highlight how stubborn is our nature and how deeply committed we are to independent courses of existence. We must learn, if we are to be secure people, how to be God-dependent rather than self-dependent. Nothing, I believe, can be more important than this.

Too often, however, we look elsewhere for the meeting of those deep spiritual needs. We develop strategies in our thinking that cause us to go in other directions in an attempt to have our basic needs met.

Just look inside your heart and you will discover the tendency which, since the Fall, is in all of us – the disposition to find our

identity and source of life in ways other than God. Then when a crisis hits us or someone or something we trusted lets us down, we begin to realise that we have put our dependency for inner security in the wrong place. We discover, often through the pain of disappointment, that there is only One on whom we can fully rely to keep us secure in the fast-flowing currents of life. No one and nothing can give us the deep security for which our heart craves, other than our heavenly Father.

What kind of strategies do women adopt, outside of God, in the hope that we will find the fulfilment that our hearts long for? What alternative routes do we pursue to find what we believe will make us secure?

An increasingly appealing route for women today is a career. Many set for themselves the goal of achievement, status or business success, and when that goal is not reached, some experience not just disappointment but devastation. When a woman builds her identity around the work that she does, if it happens that she is fired or made redundant, her sense of identity can easily collapse. Our identity ought never to be found in what we do, but rather in who we are. And who are we? We are daughters of the living God, the objects of His tender and loving care, washed in His blood and guaranteed a future with Him in eternity. When our identity is in God and we are aware that He has designed us for a specific purpose, then understanding and surrendering to that enables us to be all we are meant to be at home, in the workplace or in the Church.

In the early 1990s I became a manager at CWR (the only woman manager at that time) and I have to admit I enjoyed a certain kudos as a result. CWR is the kind of organisation where "constant change is here to stay" and in due time there was a period of restructuring when our CEO decided that we did not need managers any more. I remember exploring my feelings at the time. One day I was a manager and the next I wasn't. I said to myself: "Jeannette, now where's your security and identity?" It took me time to think it through, although I understood and taught the principles I am writing about here. It helped me see, first-hand, the peril of building your identity around what one does rather than who one is.

Another – perhaps more subtle – route we may go down to have our basic needs met is that of our physical appearance. I don't think there's anything wrong in a woman wanting to make the best of her appearance but it is so easy to spend time and money on clothes and other things in an attempt to feel emotionally intact.

Yet another escape route down which we can travel is that of a shopping spree. You've heard the saying, I am sure, "When the going gets tough, the tough go shopping." On looking back I found this to be so in my own life a few years ago when, after an interview with my surgeon agreeing the date of my operation for cancer of the colon, I drove straight into the nearby town and bought myself a handbag!

When we look into Scripture we are reminded in a host of places that appearance, wealth, possessions, and achievement are not where life is to be found. Life is found in Christ, not in the abundance of things we possess (Luke 12:15).

Sometimes it is our church-related activities that become a self-serving route instead of a God-serving one. Perhaps we live to hear such statements as these: "No one runs the Children's Church like you do. Oh, you are such a tireless and industrious soul!" Without realising it, our activities and responsibilities can soon become the focus of our attention and, slowly but surely, we can become more taken up with working for God and impressing others than actually worshipping Him.

We ought regularly to ask ourselves: "Is God the primary object of my devotion and service, or am I more concerned with the things of God than with God Himself?" And when, because we are unappreciated, we become discouraged, it might be helpful to ask ourselves the question: "Was the expectation of appreciation the motivation of my service?"

And consider this also – other people, too, can monopolise our time in a way that pushes God out. It's quite easy for another person to become the focus of our lives, especially another Christian person. It might be our prayer partner, our house group leader or even our minister with whom we get caught up. It may begin over a spiritual matter but we may draw too close to that person in a way that is inappropriate and unwise.

It might also be family members – our husband, parents or children – from whom we try to draw our life and sense of identity. We try to live through them and their activities and achievements. How it points to the fact that if we do not draw deeply from God in order that we can minister to our loved ones, then we will finish up manipulating them to give to us, rather than our giving to them.

It needs to be understood that there is a right way to position these people and things in our lives, but also a wrong way. Isaiah 44:14–17 explains this well. It speaks of a man who "plants a pine, and the rain nourishes it. Then it shall be for a man to burn, for he will take some of it and warm himself; yes, he kindles it and bakes bread; indeed he makes a god and worships it ..." (NKJ). So he cuts down the tree, uses half for the fire but the other half he uses to make an idol to worship. How foolish, we think, that a person can act in this way! Yet how often do we act in a similar way ourselves?

Maybe we won't know how much we depend on something and have made it into an idol until it's not there any more. Maturity is displayed in where we put our dependency. The mature person places dependency not in things or people but in God Himself. The sooner we realise this, the better. Otherwise we may engage in unhealthy relationships, searching for acclaim in frantic volunteer work, seeking attention with newer and niftier designer clothes, manipulating children towards perfection, and so on. None of these endeavours will satisfy the longings we have in the centre of our souls. They are just substitutes to try to fill the place that only God can fill. We do not need other people or things to hold us. God can hold us "no matter what".

What steps can we take to help us find our real security in God, to put our dependency and trust in Him? I have found the following steps to be helpful in my own life as I have set out to find my security in God. I hope they will be helpful to you, too.

1. *Face the fact that you cannot make your life work on your own.* Be aware that deep down in your heart, embedded like splintered glass, is a stubborn commitment to independence. It may only be when things go wrong that you turn in desperation to God. But every one of us must come to terms with the fact that whether things go well or not, we cannot make our lives work independently of God. We see DIY shops in nearly every shopping precinct these days. To many of us, *do it yourself* comes naturally not only in running our homes but in running our lives also.

2. *Be willing to face and enter into your disappointments.* When things go wrong in life, how often do we protect ourselves from feeling the depth of the disappointment by use of the strategy of denial to put distance between what has happened and the full force of our emotional pain?

When Princess Diana died, one mother said in a television interview that when she told her little girl, the child responded, "I don't have to believe it, if I don't want to." Like that little girl, we can pretend that we are not really affected by something. It's a way of coping without the necessity of having to depend on God. But if we can say "yes" to the pain, we can discover how wonderfully real God becomes to us in those situations. We can experience His healing touch more deeply and, because we are being more honest and real, it opens the way to experiencing greater heights of joy, too.

3. *Determine to forgive everyone who has ever hurt you.* One of the reasons why we often find it difficult to forgive someone is because we have depended on them, rather than God, to come through for us. Unconsciously, we may have allowed another person to take up the central place that God requires for Himself.

To put it another way, if our sense of worth is bound up in how people relate to us and they let us down, it becomes very difficult to forgive them fully. One of the things we often fail to realise is that forgiveness is a process and begins with our response to the biblical command to forgive.

Someone has described forgiveness like peeling an onion. Tears will probably be shed at different stages. But keep going, complete forgiveness is possible and at the end of the process, there lies the place of freedom for your soul.

4. *Repent of self-protective strategies and trust God to be your source of security.* Repentance is very important in developing security, and in order to repent effectively each one of us needs to ask ourselves some *serious* questions, such as:

- What is the main strategy on which I depend to make my life work?
- What keeps me away from my pain?
- Who or what may be my idols?
- How do I go about getting my needs met?
- Who or what is at the centre of my life, in the place God has designed for Himself?

Once we discover that we are not depending upon God for our security then the only way to deal with that is through radical repentance. We must seek His forgiveness for our misplaced dependency. There can be no real growth in the area of security until this is clearly recognised. We can't move on with God into the future until things of the past have been put right.

5. *Realise that security begins with a belief, not a feeling.* Our feelings follow our beliefs, like little ducks follow their mother on a pond. This is why we should be more concerned with beliefs than feelings. Remind yourself constantly that you are secure in Christ, until that belief takes root in your soul. In relation to feelings, however, we must always be willing to acknowledge them; not deny them and pretend we do not feel anxious, disappointed or angry, when we do. But having acknowledged our feelings, it is crucial that we then choose to do the right thing.

6. *Give yourself to that belief and be willing to be vulnerable.* The fact that we have a firm belief that our security is in God does not mean we will not feel hurt when other people let us down or do not come through for us. But, nevertheless, we have to put ourselves on the line and trust in God. Being vulnerable means that we are willing to come to terms with our human frailty and admit to feelings of vulnerability, yet at the same time give ourselves to the Lord and say with the psalmist, "God is the strength of my heart" (Psalm 73:26).

My prayer is that these steps will set you on the path to becoming a woman who is secure in God and that you will walk that path until it becomes instinctive and that you will come to know it, like you know your way home.

CHAPTER TWO

# LIFE CENTRE:
# A DREAM COME TRUE

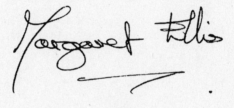

# Biography

Margaret is a qualified teacher who has been involved in the leadership of Revelation Church in West Sussex and Hampshire for many years. She is currently Project Manager for Life Centre, a charity providing support for survivors of rape and sexual abuse. She works as a face-to-face counsellor herself within Life Centre and also oversees the telephone counselling service it provides. She combines this work with providing psychosexual therapy within a clinic in the local hospital. Margaret also has a preaching ministry.

I was the main leader of the original congregation of Revelation Church in Chichester and part of the team overseeing our other congregations. I loved seeing all types of people released in ministry, making room for the creative in our worship and finding ways as a church to be good news to our community. My vision has always been expressed through the church and I have been privileged to be part of a spiritual community that has given me endless space to initiate and dream.

I was discipling a young adult on a year-long Christian team, who I will call "Chrissy". She was so on fire for God, she was an inspiration to me. With a maturity beyond her years and a deep passion for Jesus, she was a leader among her peers. The doorbell rang for her weekly tutorial and in walked a crumpled shell of her former self.

I can still see her lost in my armchair, hugging her knees with her head down. She was like a beautiful seabird, covered in tar, frightened, confused and muzzled. Through chasms of silence she told me facts that had disrupted her life in the space of a week. A guy she had known for years had given her a lift home after a group from the church had been out for the evening. In the car he raped her – twice. She shouted, kicked, repeated "*No!*", but he had his relentless way. It was horrific.

She decided that she wanted to go to the police to try and stop him from doing it again. After hours of the most intrusive questions and medical examinations of her injuries (by a male doctor), she was turned out on the streets with a phone number for counselling support three counties away. On investigation, workers at this rape crisis centre were unable to see her anyway as she lived outside of their funded area. Her case also didn't even get to court.

Our tutorials abandoned discussing essays and finer points of evangelism; instead we slowly worked through the trauma, nightmares, anger, guilt, fears and new world that had been born.

She wrote this:

> I lay on my bed at home after I had been raped in a lot of pain physically. I don't think I have ever felt so alone, hurt, dirty and guilty. It was just horrific. A few days later I told a friend. As she hugged me I felt like I was going to break. She prayed for me and out of my brokenness and desperation I felt God's presence like never before. I felt his angels around me, I felt safe in his arms, it was like he was carrying me through the pain. Over the next months I worked through the issues of feeling guilty and dirty, anger, blame and feeling completely crushed. I gave up on trying to work out the "Why?" because I don't think I will ever know.
>
> Why am I telling you? Because too often the victims remain silent and let themselves be eaten up by guilt and shame. I want anybody who has been the subject of any kind of abuse to know that God can heal anything.

For me, it was as though a stone had been thrown into my lake that would never reach the bottom. The ripples had to affect my community. It wasn't enough to support Chrissy. What about all the other men and women outside of the church who would be given a useless phone number and left to fend for themselves? God started to birth a dream in me to set up a centre where people who had been sexually violated in any way – be it as children or adults – could receive the support they deserved. If it was going to reach the wider community, it had to be done professionally.

Looking back on my pastoral history, I realised I actually had a lot of experience of supporting survivors of sexual abuse. What I didn't have was secular qualifications. So I signed up at a nearby university and over the next few years gained a general counselling qualification, as well as a diploma and postgraduate qualification in psychosexual counselling and therapy. I also did all the in-house training for another rape crisis service and worked as a volunteer counsellor for them for two years.

There were times during the psychosexual training that I had to pinch myself to believe this was really me. Brought up in a loving home by missionary parents, here I was learning about every form of sexual paraphilia and dysfunction that would grace a psychosexual clinic! I went on a steep learning curve and had to hang on to God for dear life. But all the time, He kept reinforcing my dream.

A year or so into my training a guy with a prophetic ministry visited our church. I had been asking God for a name for the centre I was dreaming of starting. He started to prophesy and my heart broke again as I heard these words:

> The Holy Spirit says you are going to have a life centre, where you restore people back to life. You will have young ladies and young men whose lives are dark, on the verge of committing suicide, who have gone through several abortions, been raped many times, abused by their fathers and mothers, no life ... there is going to be a Life Centre here. You will take people and nurse them back to life. It will be a place where people get rid of their shame. It'll be a place where Isaiah 61 will come to pass. They get their

life back, they get their childhood back, they get their youth back, they get their families back, they get their reputation back, they get their purity back, they get their self-worth back at the Life Centre.

And so it was named.

As I came to the end of my training, a team of us started work for real to bring the vision to reality. Life Centre was registered as a charity; volunteers were recruited and trained to staff the telephone counselling line; we set policies and procedures in place. As I write, we have had a telephone counselling line open for one month. We have already had calls from survivors themselves, as well as from those close to them who need some support as they care for their partner, child or friend who has suffered the trauma of rape or other forms of sexual abuse. We are also able to provide face-to-face counselling for those who wish to come into the centre. Money is gradually coming through from the council and other statutory agencies, although the funding is a constant step of faith.

I have started to speak out about these issues in churches around the country. So much silence shrouds sexual issues in Christian culture. I let it be known at Spring Harvest (a large interdenominational conference in the UK), that I now work as a psychosexual therapist and was moved by the numbers of men and women of all ages who wanted to talk about their sexual problems. Many had not been abused, but were unhappy sexually for a multitude of reasons. We need as Christians to go so much further than defining the fences of our sexual ethics. What about all the joys, challenges and skills involved in gardening within the fence?

But once the silence is shattered, then the challenge comes as to how constructively to respond to someone who has been through sexually abusive experiences. I have been asked this many times, and also heard many horror stories of survivors being further damaged by the ignorant and thoughtless responses of people in their churches.

Imagine the prison of childhood for Alex who was sexually abused by her father, the vicar of their middle-class, Anglican Church. After eleven years of footsteps on the stairs leading to the stifling sensations to body and mind of his vilely abusive sexual acts, she broke her silent prison and told a trusted member of the church. Imagine the crushing sense of inevitability when she saw the look of disbelief on this person's face, followed through with their words and actions, and how she climbed back into her only shell of protection: a fantasy world that would undo her own future. She expressed her vulnerability and deep feelings by writing tragically descriptive poems such as this one:

Daddy, Don't

*Slut me*
*Cut me*
*Slice me*
*Dice me*

*Call me*
*Maul me*
*Bruise me*
*Use me*

*Prick me*
*Pin me*
*Thump me*
*Pump me*

*Need me*
*Bleed me*
*Please, just leave me.*

Imagine the muscly man who spoke to me at the end of a Christian meeting who was night after night being attacked in his sleep by his wife, leaving him with broken bones and embarrassing bruises to explain to his workmates. He once called the police only to be arrested himself as it was filed as a domestic violence call.

How should we respond if an adult discloses sexual (or physical) abuse to us? My first principle is always to believe. You will cause huge damage if you don't believe and it is true; minimal damage if you do believe and it is not true. Don't shut them down or give the message that you can't hear, however painful the listening. Let them tell you more if they want to. There will always be more than what they tell you.

Let them know that you do not see it as their fault. Even if there are contributory factors, they did not ask to be abused or raped.

If a child discloses abuse you need to be aware of child protection issues. Explain that you will need to tell some other people about this in order to try and protect them. Let them know that you believe them and that it is not their fault.

Child abuse is against the law of our land and therefore not a matter to be settled purely with church authority. If a murder had been committed it could not be left with the church leaders to resolve. If you felt a case of abuse was being covered up by church leadership, you have a right and a duty to take it to social services or the police yourself. The Bible is clear that we should submit to the just laws of our land.

With both adults and children, try to see beyond your own feelings of helplessness – know that what you cannot give is OK. They most likely know that already, and they still picked you to talk to. Don't feel you need to have answers or "know what to say". That probably wouldn't help anyway.

What you can give is *love*: unconditional acceptance and believing in the beauty within them. This is Christ.

What you can give is the power of *listening*. In one of our Life Centre counselling rooms, we have a large pair of lips made out of plaster by someone I was counselling. She set in the lips a red zip, mostly tight shut, with just the first few teeth of the zip opening.

Another much-loved person writes:

> What sometimes sounds like a booming voice in your head is actually a quiet whisper on your lips. When I couldn't speak I let my starving body shout for me. I let the blood from my self-inflicted wounds tell of my hurt and anger. I had to speak, had to find the voice of a 5-year-old fighting inside me to express itself or I would implode.
>
> I formed three little words but not the ones that everyone wants to hear. I've never felt the room so big, myself so small, my face so red and my voice so loud.
>
> "Dad abused me."
>
> It hung in the air, the world paused and I waited for the sky to cave in, for chaos to occur, the judge to condemn me, the gunshot to fire.
>
> Nothing, silence, nothing.
>
> One year on and I am still looking at the sky and wondering why it looks so stable. I have a voice. That knowledge, that reality, is one of – if not the most – freeing, life-changing and healing facts that I have ever discovered.
>
> And as I speak, I watch that child with fluffy, blonde hair and big, sad, blue eyes as she turns her back and shuts the front door, only stopping to open the letter box and shout *"No, no, no, no, no!"* until it echoes and vibrates through every corner, every nook and cranny of the house that she was silenced in.

What you can give is to let them be in the place where they are, without you forcing them on beyond what they are ready for. This is uncomfortable. We may want them to feel clean, but they need to express the dirt that has stuck on them. We may want them to know the releasing power of forgiveness, but they may need to express their anger as Jesus does in Revelation 19:15 as He treads the winepress of the wrath of God Almighty. Church communities tend to be places that don't welcome anger. We usually prefer our members to suppress their anger and turn it instead into depression. This we can nurture and that is pastoral. Nurturing feels good. Anger is scary, bad, unchristian. And yet the anger of God shouts at us through the pages of Scripture, despite being barred from many of our churches.

God gave me a dream for Life Centre. Dreams really can come true.

William Booth spoke of his own dream to transform the squalor of London through evangelism and social transformation. He wrote: "The call came from Heaven; but the call came from humanity as well."

What cries do you hear from heaven; what cries do you hear from humanity around you?

"If you have faith as small as a mustard seed, you can say to this mountain, 'move from here to there' and it will move. Nothing will be impossible for you." So Jesus eggs us on. What dreams could God birth in you?

If you would like to phone the Life Centre counselling line, please feel free to phone any Thursday or Sunday evening on 01243 779196.

CHAPTER THREE

# Building
## a House of Prayer

Faith Forster

# Biography

Faith Forster has been involved in Christian ministry and leadership for many years alongside her husband, Roger, who is the founder and leader of Ichthus Christian Fellowship. Faith preaches, teaches and pastors, and also serves on a number of boards and councils; in particular, the UK Evangelical Alliance, Spring Harvest and the World Evangelical Fellowship. She believes passionately in the power of prayer and the Word of God, and loves to see lives transformed by these means. A dynamic speaker, Faith inspires and encourages all those that hear her words of experience and conviction.

"My house shall be called a house of prayer for all nations." These words were running over and over in my mind as I stood in the driveway of the rather dilapidated property we had just bought. The year was 1988. Fourteen years earlier, my husband Roger and I, together with a group of friends, had launched a new church plant, which we called Ichthus Christian Fellowship, in South East London where we lived.

In those beginning years we had intensively evangelised the area, visiting homes, befriending local people, offering practical help in a variety of ways to the people of our inner-city "parish". We grew rapidly from a small group of about 14 people, to a large church with numerous congregations. We also supported overseas mission and had now become a sending church with our own mission thrusts and personnel. Our prayer needs were vast.

In 1977 we had bought a large Edwardian house in Forest Hill as a base for fellowship and training. Now, 11 years on, the property next door had come on the market. The owners had given us first option to buy, as it would be an obvious way to expand our base and activities. When, as a group of leaders, we went around the house before purchasing, we began discussing what specific use the Lord had in mind for the house. We had already talked about our need for a place of prayer at the heart of our work. Roger had long been inspired by the story of the Moravian 24-hour prayer meetings that turned into a hundred years of prayer! As we stood in the house in one of the large rooms, God spoke to me very clearly.

It was as if I could see the words written on a scroll around the walls, "My house shall be a house of prayer for all nations."

Now, having bought the property, we had to decide how to put these words into practice. I soon began to feel God pushing me to organise and lead a prayer ministry, based in the house. I have always been a bit of a gap-filler so I naturally felt concerned to fill the prayer gap that had began to emerge as our work had become larger and more widely spread. But even so, I felt totally inadequate to teach or lead others in prayer.

How seldom God worries about our inability to do what He calls us to do! He knows better than we do that we really can do nothing without Him, but with Him all things are possible. Besides, I had learned a thing or two about prayer through the "school of hard knocks" (which is always where we learn most). In 1982, for example, we had faced the biggest family crisis of our lives, when our 15-year-old son, Chris, was diagnosed with acute lymphatic cancer. This had spread rapidly into his spinal fluid and thus to the central nervous system. His prognosis had been extremely poor but God laid a strong spirit of intercession on us and as we cried out to Him we received a miracle. Chris was healed as rapidly as he had become ill. He has stayed free of cancer ever since. But we learned more during that time about the wiles and ways of our enemy, Satan, and about the powerful love and work of God than we could ever have dreamed.

A few years later, we were once again pouring ourselves out in prayer – this time for one of our daughters, who was going through a period of teenage turmoil and confusion, not wholly unconnected with the trauma of her brother's illness. Once again we learned how to prevail before God in intercession and to lay hold of His promises of restoration until we saw them fulfilled. Once the prayer house was up and running, prayer targets like these – for the crises and family needs of our church members and others – became commonplace.

As I recall the birth and emergence of our Ichthus prayer ministry, my heart goes out in gratitude to God for the wonderful women and men whom God called to work alongside us in prayer. The majority of our intercessors were, and are, women. This is not because men don't pray (we have some fine male prayer leaders), but because women often have an intuitive nature suited to prayer and listening to God, and they can often find some time in their day to intercede, in between running their homes and cooking, chauffeuring for their children and doing household tasks. When we stand in glory, I believe we will see a great multitude of radiant, glorious saints who were the pray-ers here on earth – who drove back the forces of hell, who brought peace to troubled situations, who prayed back the prodigals from their wanderings, who stood like an armed guard around God's servants and ministers.

How I thank God for women like Ruth, our first prayer administrator, whose artistic giftings, sensitivity, hard work, love for people and relational skills did so much to draw our intercession base together and to encourage and facilitate me in what I was trying to achieve. I think also of Liz, my ministry assistant at first, who soon became not only my colleague, but also my close friend and prayer partner. Together we prayed into many seemingly hopeless situations and saw them turn round; we prayed for each other's families and saw God do such gracious things for our loved ones. What a precious partnership we had for eight and a half years, until unexpectedly God brought along her Prince Charming, a godly widower, and she was whisked off to Sweden to become a pastor's wife and mother to a ready-made family.

Then there is Eila. After many years of pioneering work overseas with her husband, Trevor, she found herself based in London with us, while Trevor, continued his Bible translation work from Britain. Some women would have grasped the opportunity to have a well-earned rest and become a lady of leisure, but not Eila. She immediately recruited herself to organise and spearhead our prayer for missions. I wonder if our overseas workers will ever know how much they owe to Eila and others like her, who poured their hearts and energy into praying protection, blessing and fruitfulness over all our workers and their families.

I will also mention Val – a wife, and mother of six children – who pioneered our borough prayer strategy. She gathered a group of women who became "watchmen" over their London borough. To detail the remarkable change in this borough over the years would take more room than is available here. But I could sum it up by saying that in 1991 it was described as "the rottenest borough" by a national newspaper because of the appalling state of its housing, schools, local government, crime, racial tensions, etc. Ten years on it is an increasingly desirable place to live, and has the highest statistics for churchgoing in the country. During all those years Val and her friends were praying weekly in shopping centres and outside schools, the town hall, the police station, etc. We saw situation after situation turning round from hopeless to hopeful and the whole area change. God is a God of hope and there is nothing too hard for Him!

Together, Ruth, Liz, Eila, Val and myself forged the prayer ministry for Ichthus, leading prayer journeys overseas as well as praying around London. On one occasion we were contacted by one of our church members, a policeman. He told us that escalating tensions between the National Front and the anti-Nazi league were expected to come to a head the next day when it was anticipated that hundreds of people on an anti-Nazi march were expected to engage with NF demonstrators gathering near their headquarters. All police leave across London had been cancelled for the next day as the police were expected to stand between the two "armies" of people and hold them apart. Major violence was predicted. We immediately drove to the spot in South London where the confrontation was expected. Having driven along the route of the planned march and noting home-owners and shopkeepers boarding up their windows in readiness for the riots, we were appalled, and burdened by God to engage more fully in prayer for this violent situation. Because it was daytime and there was heavy traffic, we decided to return late that evening to pray along the route on foot.

Just before midnight we were back in the area, accompanied by the Christian policeman. It was just as well he was with us, as the area was now completely cordoned off by the police, and we were only allowed in because he vouched for us. We prayed for peace and for a restraining of violence and evil. We prayed that the power of the cross of Jesus would bring peace the next day. At the point of the route where the police line would be and where the two opposing factions were predicted to engage in violent confrontation, we took a vial of olive oil and placed minute drops of anointing oil at intervals across the road, asking that the presence of God's Spirit would be there to protect and deliver from evil. Then, with a sense of peace that we had done what God had asked us to do, we went home to bed.

The next day, everything started out as expected at first. Huge crowds began massing for the two demonstrations but as the march drew nearer, the police, possibly acting on a tip-off, found a number of caches of petrol bombs and other weapons and confiscated them. When the demonstrations began, and the police were seeking to "hold the line" against the surging tide of aggressive people, the line did in fact hold and, although there were scuffles and skirmishes, there was no major injury or violence. Watching it on television, I could only give glory and thanks to our faithful God.

This was just one of the many occasions when we prayed into our inner-city problems and threats and found God bringing peace and order. (We didn't often accompany our prayers with prophetic acts, as on this occasion, because such actions are only valuable if they are directly inspired by God.)

As you will have gathered, I believe in prayer! I believe every one of us can engage with God and find Him getting His will done through our intercession, whether our cry is on behalf of our family or for our community.

I find that many people don't pray because they don't have confidence that God hears their prayers. In the Bible there is a story in the life of Elijah (1 Kings 17) where a woman faces a crisis in her home. Her son has become acutely ill and has died and she cries out in pain and distress to Elijah. Elijah, who is held up as an example of an ordinary person who knew how to pray (James 5:17), saved the situation. But the woman's initial reaction to the crisis revealed three primary reasons why we often find it hard to pray. When the woman saw her lifeless son she cried out to Elijah, "What do you have against me, man of God? Did you come to remind me of my sin and kill my son?" (1 Kings 17:18).

There are three major thought habits and beliefs that are revealed in this little speech that will always hinder our prayers until we deal with them! The first is: "God is against me", or at least: "He is not for me." Many people live without any sense of love or affirmation from God. They do not live in a conscious place of God's blessing and commitment toward them. Therefore whenever something goes wrong they think, "That's it. I knew it. God doesn't love me. He hates me. He doesn't want to help me." If you believe this in your heart you are unlikely to pray the kind of bold, faith-filled prayers that Elijah did. Sometimes our problem is that we have never felt loved or affirmed in our lives and therefore find it hard to believe in God's affirmation. At other times, this sense of blessing is stolen from us by the enemy, and his oppression. Whichever it is, we need to find someone to pray with us for healing in this area so that we can believe the truth, which is that God is longing to help us, to act for us, to save us. He is always kind and merciful.

The second underlying thought-habit here is: "I am guilty. I deserve this catastrophe because I have sinned." This is another stronghold of the mind that Satan loves to lock us into. If we feel guilty, we will accept whatever bad thing the enemy wants to put our way. The answer is to distinguish between true guilt and false guilt, although both of them are dealt with by the blood of Jesus. Through His death, Jesus delivers us from the guilt and consequences of our sin and also from the accusations that the devil would throw at us. The Accuser has been thrown down, we are told in the book of Revelation (Rev. 12:10–11). If you feel guilty all the time you will find it hard to pray at all; except perhaps for yourself, and even then not with faith. You need to know that Jesus died for you and that "if we confess our sins, he is faithful and just and will forgive us our sins and purify us from all unrighteousness" (1 John 1:9). We come to God, not on the basis of our righteousness but of His. Let's ask Him to help us deal with our guilt today, and discover the power of His blood to set us free.

The third thought-habit is that of hopelessness. "It's all hopeless. Nothing will change. Why bother to pray about it?" This is a very insidious stronghold, because it affects us in small matters as well as great. It is of course a form of fatalism, which is really unbelief. We do not really believe in a God who is alive and active, who hears prayer and who will answer. Possibly at heart we don't believe at all! It is a good thing to challenge our own unbelief. What do we really believe God can/will do? The woman in the story of Elijah was absolutely without hope about the outcome of her tragic situation, but fortunately Elijah wasn't. He snatched the boy from her, took him up to his own room and cried out to the God he knew so well. Faith grows out of relationship with God. As Elijah exerted himself in prayer and in action over the boy, God heard his prayer, the boy's life was restored to him, and the boy was restored alive to his mother. What a gracious, compassionate God we have!

But this story challenges me as I hope it will challenge you. What hidden hopelessness, guilt or lack of trust lurks in my own heart to hinder my prayers? Let's ask God to heal our hearts and deliver us from unbelief, so that we are able to pray effectively not just for our own families, but for the even greater needs of others. I am looking to see a great army of warriors in prayer raised up, women who will know their God, who will deal with unbelief by laying hold of God's word, and who will through faith "conquer kingdoms, administer justice and gain what was promised" (Heb. 11:33).

This is an exciting calling. Will you join me?

CHAPTER FOUR

# THE BINDS AND BLESSINGS
# OF BEING A WORKING WOMAN

*Michele Guinness*

# Biography

Brought up in a Jewish family, converted as a teenager and married to an Anglican clergyman, Michele Guinness is a freelance journalist and PR consultant. She has worked as a researcher, writer and presenter for most major British television companies and for BBC Radio 2 and 4.

She is currently communications lead for the North West Lancashire Teenage Pregnancy Campaign and also involved in communication training.

As well as contributing regularly to a variety of magazines, she has written: *Child of the Covenant*, her autobiography; *Promised Land*, the story of a Yorkshire mining town during the strike; *Tapestry of Voices*, meditations on women's lives; *A Little Kosher Seasoning*, exploring how Christians can discover their Jewish roots; *Made for Each Other: Reflections on the Opposite Sex*, looking at how men and women relate to each other – or don't! *Woman: The Full Story* was published last year.

Michele lives in Lancaster where her husband, Peter is vicar of St Thomas'. They have two children, Joel aged 24 and Abby aged 21.

There were three mature, experienced ministers' wives on the panel that evening at the ministers' training college, as we, nervous, soon-to-be-in-their-shoes, little women waited in anticipation for the glimmers of wisdom that would light our pathway into an unknown and rather scary future.

"Don't worry your husband with your minor problems about running the home and the children. He is doing the work of God. Release him to fulfil his ministry."

Each said the same. By the third repeat I was on my feet. "I didn't know we were called to be doormats," I heard myself saying, in the embarrassed hush. "I thought marriage was about each releasing the other to fulfil our God-given calling and potential."

I can't recall the panel's reply, only the dismissive reaction of the other student wives. "We always knew you were a radical and a feminist."

Was I? Not consciously. The two years I had worked as a detached youth worker before my marriage had certainly given me an awareness of the demoralising effects of social exclusion. It seemed to me that the exploitation or diminishing of one human being at the cost of another was not the gospel of freedom Christ preached, but politically, I was still fairly conservative, the well-educated daughter of a fairly well-heeled Jewish family.

As for women's issues, though they were exercising the minds of many of the female students in those heady days of the early 1980s as they fought for the right to be ordained, and

though my instinctive sense of fairness placed me on their side, I certainly hadn't thought it through theologically. In fact, converted as a teenager, a member of a free evangelical church for most of my early Christian life, I was, till that moment, fairly traditional in my views on that subject too.

Only six years earlier I had sat with Peter in a café shortly before our marriage, the love light shining in my eyes, and said, "I won't go out to work. I will stay at home and iron your shirts and darn your socks." Given the way things turned out, we laugh about it now.

I think I imagined living in a gingerbread cottage, with honeysuckle growing up the wall, and clean, sweet-smelling nappies wafting gently in the breeze as they hung out to dry in the summer sun. In reality, the baby years were my wilderness years. If one person had told me I would make a better mother of teenagers than babies, it would have released me from the guilt induced by the stifling and restless boredom I felt. But blessed with the ministry of encouragement, Christians simply said, "Just wait, it gets worse."

To get my head and hands out of the nappy bucket, I began to write radio scripts. They were accepted, and I was asked for more, so whenever the children were at playschool or asleep – at lunchtime, in the evening, in the early hours of the morning – I slaved over a hot word processor. One day I said to God, in that state of semi-reverie praying can be, "When the children are older, you know what I'd really like to do? Become a television researcher."

Abby had been at school full-time for a month when the phone rang, and the Head of Religion at Central Television offered me a job as a researcher.

"What'll we do with the children after school? How will we manage?" I said to Peter.

"We will," he reassured me. "I can be at home doing administration, and if I can't, someone will help out."

I sat at an empty desk on my first morning back at work, terrified out of my wits, totally devoid of self-confidence, having pushed a pram, not a blank piece of paper around for the past seven years. Slowly, the creative ideas began to flow, but some strange law governing the universe of working women seemed to dictate that as my professional skills grew, my home-making skills declined.

Peter and I were both totally committed to hospitality, but that meant rearranging our relationship as well as sharing the chores.

"I've cleaned the floor for you," he said one night.

"No!" I shouted in exasperation, "you haven't done it for me, you've done it for us. This is our home."

"Oh, yes," he said ruefully, as the implications of our new life and shared ministry finally dawned.

I couldn't begin to imagine how single people coped, running a home and a job in tandem, on their own. Without Peter's full support and encouragement, without his conviction that it was God's intention that I should have as much opportunity to fulfil my call as he had to fulfil his, even if it meant minding the home fires while I was away filming, I could not have gone on. No wonder only 9 per cent of women said in a recent survey that they would work full-time, given the choice – especially as 60 per cent still did most of the housework.

I left all the financial accounting and DIY to Peter, because it bored me silly. He left the cooking to me, because he hated it so much. I insisted, however, that he came and peeled potatoes and chopped carrots, not because I didn't want to be a skivvy, but because it was our only opportunity to talk. Even so, my

cooking, all last-minute, was not what it had once been, and for a Jewish woman it was hard not to be Mrs Perfect in the kitchen.

Occasionally, my gem of a mother-in-law, who lived around the corner, implied that her son and grandchildren were not being adequately cared for. Some church members let me know they would have preferred a minister's wife who was there for them. Others hinted darkly at the long-term damage to children of working mothers, and one told me in no uncertain terms that the church could have understood my doing a caring job like nursing or teaching – acceptable professions for a Christian – but not an unproductive and glamorous job in the media. I sat in the bath at night in a state of exhaustion and shouted to all my critics, "I do not need your approval. I only need God's, and I know He approves of me."

I didn't always feel I deserved it. The job wasn't glamorous. Most of it was spent in that great institution, the British office, and I often found myself drawn unwittingly into the criticisms of the boss, the bitching among the colleagues, and the intrigues that are an integral part of any closed environment. Every day I asked God to guard my tongue, and guide me through the shark-infested waters, to protect me from the flattering advances of attractive men, and the temptation to jostle for promotion. Looking back, I think I was too keen to please, too nice and too passive – a terrible womanly weakness.

I submitted to the sexual harassment of one of the directors because he was a Christian, and I assumed that was what Christians did. I didn't know then that when Jesus talked of turning the other cheek He was advocating passive resistance. A master would only slap a slave with the palm of his hand. For a slave to offer him the other side of the face as well would disarm him completely. In the end, the director tried it on with a non-Christian and, rightly, was suspended at once. The duty to protect my colleagues had never occurred to me. It was some time before I learned to be more assertive – in Christian terms, to have the courage to do what God required, whatever the risk, whatever the cost, like some of the great women of the Bible, but it's a hard lesson to learn.

After two years I moved to the BBC to present a daily local radio programme. When the station manager who hired me was promoted and replaced by another, determined to move his own cronies in, my days were numbered. It was a terrible blow to my pride, and a financial worry. A minister's pay is not substantial, and we had been on family income supplement before I started work. Nonetheless, I realised I had a choice – to put myself in the hands of the station manager and rail against the injustice of it all, or put myself in the hands of God, believing He knew, and may even have planned, this eventuality and had an alternative in mind. The former made me feel bitter, angry and resentful; the latter filled me with peace and expectation. I knew which was the safer place. I told my boss firmly and gently that I would work out my contract, and made up my mind to clamp my jaw shut and not to criticise him to my colleagues. One by one they suffered the same fate.

"You're better out of it," my ex-PA said on the phone one night. "The atmosphere is awful – weeping and wailing and screaming in the corridors. You never did that. Was it because you're a Christian?"

At around the same time, Peter saw an advert for a job he felt was right. We were free to move. It has been fascinating to see the way at different times our different ministries have taken priority. To my immense disappointment, the doors to working in the media never opened in quite the same way

again, but an extraordinary new opportunity arose.

Our first months in the new church were extremely difficult. We tend to put our stress somewhere in our bodies, and mine obviously went into my womanly bits, for out of the blue, I was told I needed a hysterectomy. Knowing what I know now, I would have asked for more information, read all the research, demanded a second opinion, looked at the alternatives, but being a patient robs us of our right mind. We're at our weakest and most vulnerable, and allow others to make choices for us that we alone should be making.

I said as much to the nurses on the ward after my operation, and they said, "Why don't you work for the NHS? We need someone like you to empower the patients to say what they think and feel, and help medical staff communicate with them more effectively."

Within five months, without knocking on a single door, I was offered the job of press officer at the biggest hospital in Lancashire. Furthermore, I could work part-time for almost as much pay as I had earned working full-time in the media, and therefore be more available for Peter, two boisterous teenagers, the occasional speaking engagement, the local church and writing a book or two. Going out to work was a rest.

The children reassure me that far from being adversely affected by the demands of my career, they enjoyed the dimension it brought to our family life. To look at them now – strong, independent, loving young adults, deeply committed to Christ – I can believe it, and heave a sigh of relief. I can still see Abby, at five, barely able to wield a knife, sitting at the kitchen table, making her own school dinner. Oh, the guilt I felt, and the pain of leaving her, sometimes for whole weekends, when I went away on speaking engagements. "The other children complain about what their mums had put in their sandwiches," she said one day. "I can't. I made them myself." That's when she first realised there could be advantages in having independence early. "I did miss you terribly when you went away", she told me recently, "but your working has opened up so many possibilities for my life."

I hope the workplace is kinder to my daughter than it was to my generation, for I wanted to give her a better world, but I have my doubts. Over 50 years ago the Christian psychologist, Paul Tournier, thought women would change the hire-and-fire culture, because we are more collaborative and more people-centred. But it is hard to hang onto our God-given femininity when we're as susceptible to ambition and power as the men. All bosses seem to exert more pressure on their workforce to work longer hours for less pay. Perhaps it's one of the perks of growing older; perhaps it's thanks to an invaluable lesson learnt at the BBC, but I refuse to submit to that kind of blackmail these days.

When my close relationship with the chairman of the health trust, a Christian herself, began to be used by jealous colleagues as a tool to question her integrity, I felt I had no alternative but to walk. In fact, though I didn't know it at the time, I went into a new job that gave me much greater scope to train health professionals in communicating with patients.

Even as I write, somewhere inside a quiet, inner voice seems to be urging me to consider taking a new leap into the unknown by handing in my notice. This is a time of change for the NHS. Trusts are being reconstructed. I am being asked to hide information from my colleagues and the press. My integrity is on the line. Should I go? We don't have a heavy mortgage hanging around our necks. That gives freedom of choice. Yet we will have to buy a house in retirement.

"But, God, I love working in the NHS," I argue. "There is so

much more I want to do. I've made so many friends. They depend on me. So does Abby. She's still at university. We can't afford a postgraduate course for her if I walk out now."

And back comes the reply, "You know I care for your children more than you do. You know I provide financially, and that when one door closes another opens. After all we've been through together, can you still not trust Me? What is it you really fear? The loss of status, the loss of significance, the loss of independence? What are they by comparison with following Me?"

In my heart I know the truth – that whether we work in or out of the home, whether we're single or married, in Christian or secular work, well or badly paid, the boss or the minion, our first calling is not to serve the church, our children, or the workplace, all of which swallow us up before we know it, but to spread the kingdom of God. And that means living by its radical standards.

CHAPTER FIVE

# GOING FOR GROWTH

Liz Hansford

## Biography

Liz Hansford is the author of *Not a Super-Saint*, the comic diary of a minister's wife, similar in style to the Adrian Plass diaries – and just as funny! She also writes for a number of Christian and secular magazines and regularly contributes to *Thought for the Day* for Radio Ulster and *Pause for Thought* on Radio 2. Liz has an increasing speaking ministry and also teaches English. She works with "Living with Leadership" and serves on the Advisory Board of Care for Northern Ireland.

She is married to John, a Baptist pastor, and has four children, one son-in-law and a cat!

I've become increasingly conscious of my time slot here on earth: I have a limited stretch of time to work on and, if I'm honest, most of it's spent working on me! So I've been challenging myself recently and asking: What did I do with my allotted time? How well did I grow? What did I achieve? How did I live? And I've become increasingly aware that I've not always made the Christian progress I'd hoped.

Another thing I've noticed is that I haven't become any better at getting better. Somehow, I imagined that as I got older, it would get easier. Holiness would fit me like a glove, the fruits of the Spirit would be flourishing with a naturalness borne of the passing years. I used to attribute my stunted growth to insufficient discipline in Bible study and prayer. If I read the passage, answered the three questions and prayed, all would be well. I wasn't sure what was *meant* to happen as I read, but I was sure whatever it was would happen. Yes, of course Scripture has totally moulded my thinking, but I want more than my thoughts to be affected – there's a bit more to me than that! In the early days, self-discipline was my goal. If I could do more then *God* would do more.

Gradually, I've realised that while these things are important, there are other principles that are more foundational for growth. For example, all the disciples spent a more-or-less equal time with Jesus, all heard the same teaching, all were totally immersed in His lifestyle, but all did not grow equally. Thus, my "more time, more effort, more reading, more prayer" theory was scotched. Why did they grow unequally? What made a Peter different from a Judas, or indeed any of the

others whose names fade from the pages of Scripture after the Gospels?

I want us to look at some principles I see operating in Scripture that I think make a difference to our growth.

Essentially growth is *relational* and *responsive*. It is about cooperating with God in what He wants to do with you, in you and through you. And cooperation is the key. The idea isn't of a daily diet of spiritual food, much like a plant being given the right nutrients. That suggests passivity. I want us to think instead of an interactive model of growth, based not on a system of reading as a mechanical daily act, but instead listening to God and then moving. It's essentially a growth pattern based on action and responding. And it's the growth pattern we see again and again in Scripture. While meditation has its place as we listen to God, I can think of no one who just sat about, meditating and waiting for the growth to happen. They meditated, then *acted* on what God had said.

Certainly, some things happened slowly, but they nonetheless happened. For example, I suspect that Simeon and Anna in the Temple didn't do too much rushing about, but by going to the Temple at the appropriate time and waiting they had the most faith-strengthening experience imaginable; their spiritual growth rate must have soared as they became part of God's plan. If they had stayed at home and simply gone on meditating then they would have missed it all.

This relational and responsive growth pattern is about moving in harmony with God. It's as interwoven as a dance; it's like being part of the choir with God as the soloist. We are not the audience simply watching God at work, we are performers with God. This past Christmas, my daughter, Charis, and I were part of a huge choir of young people (OK, I sneaked in!) accompanying Maire Brennan, Graham Kendrick and the World Wide Message Tribe. Simply put, our job was to sing, not listen. *We are not watchers but participators*; delighting in the gifts of the Solo Artist, but absolutely focused on where He is, on tiptoe, listening for our cue, ready to create harmony with Him. Silence is not an option. If you've ever been in a musical or a play or performance you'll know what a buzz there is in being part of it all. You're the insiders, the people being watched, you work totally together as a team; and I believe God wants us to have the same buzz as we participate with Him.

You grow as you act and participate. God does not mean us to view these as two distinct stages, with action being allowed only when you've grown enough and somehow proved yourself spiritually. Spiritual infants can move with and for God, and in doing so they get stronger.

- Are you dependent on a mechanical reading and praying that does not seem to be producing fruit?
- Is your Christian growth plan responsive or passive?
- Are you looking for active ways you can cooperate with God?

I want to look now in a bit more detail at some of the aspects of responsive growth. At what it might actually look like.

## Letting Go

John reversed the car out of the drive, and in the second it took him to swing it round and turn towards the main road, little Nathan, aged three, had dashed out the gate and was helpfully "pushing" Daddy's car along the road. We lived on the corner site of a very quiet cul-de-sac; so with no traffic in sight, I stood at the front door looking over the garden wall, momentarily thinking it was just a bit of playful fun. The car rounded the bend, going up the hill towards the T-junction – but there was no sign of Nathan letting go. I watched in horror as John began to gather speed, moving much faster than Nathan's little legs could possibly run. Two things flashed across my mind as I vaulted the wall: for some reason, Nathan could not let go of the car and, secondly, John had not seen him run to the back of the car and was completely unaware that he was dragging his 3-year-old son behind him. I screamed for him to stop, louder than I've ever screamed in my life, but with the windows up John could not hear. All I could do was watch and beg, "Dear Lord, let him let go. Help him release himself. Let go, let go!" As the car swung round the second bend, the momentum flung Nathan to the other side of the road and John drove on, oblivious to all that had happened. Nathan lay in the gutter, very bruised and shaken but alive and, amazingly, with no serious injuries.

Letting go is a basic principle of growth and knowing when to let go is important.

Jean is head of home economics in a local school, and it's not hard to see why she's had a ministry in hospitality and church catering for years! This morning I had coffee with her, sampling her lighter-than-light scones and crisp pastry rhubarb tart. But recently she realised that God wanted her to let go of that ministry. She handed in her resignation as church caterer – which distinctly worried me since, as ministry wife and supposed doer of all left-over tasks, I could see the job coming my way. All I can say is, this would not have been a blessing to the congregation, since crisp pastry and I do not have much in common. But within a few months Jean found herself in an administrative and leadership position that is just right for her.

Leaving your settled task does two things: it allows God to move you on and it also allows Him to move someone else in! If I'm doing a task that God meant for someone else then I'm overworked and the "someone else" is not having the joy of being used. Sometimes others are waiting in the wings, understudies for years, whose opportunity never comes because we're hanging on. We feel secure because it's always been our slot; and we know we can do it! But perhaps God wants someone different in that space we're filling so competently. Or maybe we're holding down half a dozen jobs, feeling that strange combination of super-spiritual significance and resentment that "nobody else will do anything round here!" All we need to do is let go – appropriately and at the right time!

Growth is all about *movement* and *change*. It's about allowing God to give new gift areas. Once upon a time Barbara could sing – or so I'm told! By the time I met her, she could have got a job on top of a fire engine. But she was locked into the gifts she once had, certain that she had a "ministry in song". It didn't take too long, though, to discover that she clearly had a ministry of encouragement. Yet, every time I asked her to share at a meeting, she volunteered to sing. It was an experience not far removed from toothache. You can get trapped in a kind of spiritual security zone. But because you've always done it doesn't mean you should always keep on doing it. God can move you on.

Moses learned that the hard way. He was secure in his position as prince in Egypt. Hadn't God miraculously rescued him and put him in that role? That, he was sure, was his calling. He had a role to ease the burden of his people, to watch out for their fair treatment. It was a safe, secure, well-trodden route. But God had other ideas. New task, new territory, new dependence. For with an unfamiliar role, self-dependence flickers and God-dependence suddenly becomes very important. I suspect that may be why God sometimes does a turn about with us. *Dependence is more important for growth than competence.* It's not that God wants incompetence, but He's not impressed when we get so blasé that we don't reckon we need Him that much in order to get a particular task done.

It's important not to get trapped in a place you shouldn't be. It may be the pressure of others who reckon that because you teach day school you should teach Sunday school, or because you work in a bank you should be the treasurer. These things may apply, and they are certainly God-given gifts, but they may not be the only gifts God has given. He may have something new for you. Something that will more evidently show His glory. It's a danger zone when you find yourself only doing what you've always done.

- Ask God if He wants you to let go of anything.
- Ask Him if you've ceased depending on Him for ministry tasks.
- Ask Him if He has something else in mind for you.

Remember, He may not give you the new task till you've let go of the old one!

## Catching the Moment

It's all too easy to miss a really important moment. To wait, hesitate and then find it's gone. I want us to look at one incident in Peter's life – the day he walked on water – as an illustration of how his experience affected his growth. It was dark and stormy, not ideal conditions for testing faith, nor for taking a stroll on the sea, and it was set against an emotional background of fear rather than confidence. Not the conditions I'd choose for faith-strengthening. Peter and the other disciples saw Jesus walking on the water towards them and instantaneously Peter was on his feet. The others meanwhile waited, safe and dry, weighing up the pros and cons, uncertain and unmoving.

Once you put your foot over the edge of the boat you're committed. The next step is down, either under the water or hopefully on it. And you don't and can't know which it's going to be until after you've committed yourself. That's quite scary. And personally I'd rather know what the result was going to be before I set out. I like neat ends, tidy finishes, certainty. I think I might have remained in the boat – or I might have decided to go second! But there wasn't the chance for that. The very act of trust strengthened Peter's faith. That meant that by the time we read about Peter in the Acts he's a man who has grown because of how he responded to opportunities for growth – he took them!

If you listen to what was actually said it's pretty interesting. (It's in Matthew 14:22–32.) Peter doesn't just rush on out. He asks Jesus to ask him to walk to Him. In other words, it's only safe if Jesus gives the command. But the others miss the moment. The moment of amazing experience that I'll bet every single one of them wished later on they had had. And they could have had – if only they'd asked. You see, catching the moment doesn't always have to be at Jesus' instigation. You can ask Him to ask you to come. You can initiate the process.

I think God gives us strategic moments for growth. *Now* moments that pass. Moments when we have a chance to exercise faith and strengthen it for later. And the only time to go for growth is God's time.

I'm known for a slight tendency to err on the side of lateness, but it extends to things that just won't wait. Autumn came and went. I really did intend to plant that huge bag of daffodil bulbs I'd bought extra early, but by December I realised it was too late and I put all thoughts of them out of my head. By then I was getting behind in the Christmas preparations! Late in the spring I opened the door of the garden shed. There, poking out of holes in the giant plastic bag, was an array of daffodils in full flower, each and every one of them doing their best against the odds. I hadn't taken action when I should have and I missed out on a glorious display.

We can lose the glorious display of God's power when we fail to cooperate with Him. We will never know what we missed, though. All we'll see is a pale version of what could have been – just as I saw a miserable version of the daffodils. *We can grow weaker by not moving with Him, by not cooperating.* My job was to plant, and I didn't do it. I missed the moment of possibility.

Every experience of faith-strengthening – especially those that were personal, made Peter a different person. A person more able to be at the centre of church growth; and individual spiritual growth and numerical growth are connected. As you experience one, your drive for the other is increased. When you see what God can do in you, you tend to reach out more confident of what He can do in others.

- What might I ask Jesus to ask me to do?
- What opportunities for faith strengthening have I taken?
- Am I tuned in to recognising "now" moments?

## Stretching Out

Someone who saw incredible numerical growth and who had her faith stretched almost to breaking point was the "woman" in Isaiah 54.

> Sing, O barren woman, you who never bore a child; burst into song, shout for joy, you who were never in labour; because more are the children of the desolate woman than of her who has a husband ... Enlarge the place of your tent, stretch your tent curtains wide, do not hold back; lengthen your cords, strengthen your stakes. For you will spread out to the right and the left. (Isa. 54:1–3)

This is a passage about unexpected growth; numerical growth and emotional growth. The woman had experienced immense pain – she was rejected and childless – but God says, "Follow My plan and we'll deal with both those issues." (Have a look at vv.4–8.) "I want you to grow and flourish, I want you to be in a relationship with Me. And I'll forgive you for messing up in the past. But I don't just want you to grow personally, I want My church to grow too. Now, here's the plan. First I want you to build a nursery, enlarge the tent ready for growth, for you're going to be overrun with children. Plan for significant spiritual and numerical growth."

This woman is going to see a faith outcome *when she responds to God*. It's relational growth again! But she's got to act first. In fact she's got to build the nursery before she's even married, never mind pregnant! And the order is important. *He speaks; we respond; He acts.* We see it again and again in Scripture. God *spoke* to Moses in the burning bush, then Moses *responded* by going to Pharaoh and finally God *acted* by setting the people free. Now where do you think this process sometimes gets clogged up? All we have to do is the middle bit. It's His job to bring the growth, but we have to respond if it's to happen.

What's even more interesting is that it was the women's task to work on the tent and to make it bigger when necessary. That's a message for us today: Women, get your church ready for growth! It's OK for women to plan and take action in obedience to what God says! You don't have to leave it to the men. And in case you think differently, God hasn't finished things off where you live. He's anticipating growth, and He's anticipating *you* doing something about it with Him. In fact, in this passage He says, "Your Maker is your husband." He's in relationship with you, and together, in cooperation with Him, the church will grow. But you'd better get building! Respond, so He can act!

He knows we tend to hesitate, so He says, "Don't hold back." Go boldly because God has promised.

A Norwegian couple felt called to Niger, but could find no missionary society to send them. They felt they must respond, so they sold everything, bought a 4-wheel drive vehicle, drove from Norway to Italy, got a boat to North Africa and drove across the Sahara to Niger. They didn't know anyone there, but within six months a local man had offered to build them a home. Today, only six years later, churches have been formed, they have a Bible school, and Muslims are inviting them to their villages to speak about Jesus. That's tent-stretching in a big way; making a public commitment that you trust and believe God. But God honours such a responsive heart. Why? Because it's a heart moving, as best it knows how, in harmony with Him.

- Have I got the order right in terms of what I expect from God?
- Where might I be holding back right now?
- Am I part of tent-stretching anywhere?
- What's the next step for me?

CHAPTER SIX

# Everything Will Live
# Where the River Goes

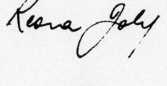

# Biography

Reona, a New Zealander, came to Europe in 1970, initially for nine months but has remained ever since! She works as a staff member for Youth with a Mission and has done so for 30 years. During that time she married Albert, the Swiss administrator, in 1981 and they moved to England. Reona has developed an acclaimed Bible teaching ministry, relating a wide range of subjects to Christian life and practice. She has a wonderful gift of being able to bring fresh insights and "life" into familiar, and sometimes overlooked, sections of the Bible. She is a source of inspiration and will have you flicking through the Scriptures with intrigue and renewed excitement! Reona's book about her pioneering visit to Albania in 1973, *Tomorrow You Die* has just been reprinted with an update on events since 1991.

In addition to being a wife and a mother, Reona travels extensively, teaching on a wide range of subjects relating to Christian life and practice.

"Would you consider speaking to our women workers at their annual retreat?" My heart leapt at this invitation. What a privilege to be with women called to serve God in a fascinating but difficult, dark Moslem land! I accepted. Some weeks later I received the theme for the retreat. Based on Ezekiel 47 would I please prepare three sessions on "The River of Life". I accepted to do this knowing it would entail lots of study and preparation.

The night before my early morning flight to attend the retreat, I packed my suitcase and my briefcase and crawled into bed around midnight. My husband stirred and said, "Everything done?"

"Everything except the message," I replied. I had tried so hard to have something to share with these wonderful women – yet nothing substantial had resulted.

"What's the subject again?" my husband asked.

"Ezekiel 47 ... the River of Life," I replied.

"Amazing," said my husband and leant over his side of the bed. "I borrowed this book this afternoon – a collection of sermons by Professor James Stewart – and look at the title: *The River of Life* ... that's the first sermon!"

"Can I take the book with me?" I pleaded, and of course my husband agreed.

During the many hours it took to travel to the retreat – by train, plane and bus – I devoured the first of James Stewart's sermons. Ezekiel 47 came alive. I had a foundation upon which to build. So many thoughts began to form in my head.

I jotted them down on bits and pieces of paper and even on my plane ticket!

Ezekiel 47 is a chapter familiar to many Christians – the prophetic vision that describes shallow water that deepened until it became a river. I had used it as an illustration when speaking about prayer. "How deep is our prayer life ...? Are the waters just at the ankles ...? Have they risen to the waist? Or are they so deep that we have to swim in them!" As I studied the chapter I realised that was an altogether inadequate interpretation. God's prophet Ezekiel is given a series of visions and from chapter 40 we learn that they began on the twenty-fifth anniversary of Judah's darkest hour – the day when Jerusalem was destroyed by Nebuchadnezzar's armies. Ezekiel was one of many rounded up, marched out through Jerusalem's gates and deported to Babylon. As a young priest he had ministered in the temple and now it was a pile of rubble and ruin. For 25 long years he lived in exile in Babylon and as Psalm 137 so poignantly declares

> By the rivers of Babylon,
> There we sat down and wept when we remembered Zion.
> How can we sing the Lord's song in a foreign land?
> If I forget you, O Jerusalem,
> May my right hand forget her skill.

Without warning, as in a dream, the Spirit of the Lord transports Ezekiel back to Judah. The city of Jerusalem stretches out before him, no longer desolate and deserted but regal, splendid and filled with people. The Temple has been rebuilt and is more magnificent than before. The glory of the Lord, which had departed 25 years previously, has not just returned, but is there ten times more powerfully.

In his vision, Ezekiel is led through the outer Temple courts to the Temple rock. There, beneath the altar of God a trickle of water rises. The water follows the path pilgrims took – left from the south side and through the Eastern Gate. The water flows from the height to the plain – from the plain to the desert – ever deepening as it goes, and everywhere it flows it brings healing and fertility and life till it bursts at last in a mighty torrent into the Dead Sea.

What a fantastic picture! For 500 yards the water is ankle-deep. For the second 500 yards it is knee-deep. For the third 500 yards it is waist-deep, and the fourth 500 yards is covered by water so deep that it has to be swum in!

What an impossible picture. How could water rise beneath the altar? How without tributaries could it deepen so rapidly? How could it get through the limestone ridge that separates East Jerusalem from the Dead Sea?

But this is not a natural river. This is God's river! This is God's stream of supernatural grace to quench a thirsting, despairing world. This is the Holy Spirit's power penetrating the arid, unreached, spiritual deserts of the world.

You say, "But in Ezekiel 47 the Holy Spirit is not mentioned." True. But consider Jesus' words in John 7:37, NASB:

> Now on the last day, the great day of the feast, Jesus stood and cried out, saying, "If anyone is thirsty, let him come to Me and drink. He who believes in Me, as the Scripture said, 'From his innermost being will flow rivers of living water.'" But this He spoke of the Spirit, whom those who believed in Him were to receive; for the Spirit was not yet given, because Jesus was not yet glorified.

There can be no doubt that the Holy Spirit provides rivers of living water to those who believe. God and God alone can

quench human thirst and bring health and healing to the
nations.

In the first century, the Church was alive with the risen life
of Jesus. Their thirst had been quenched and God's Spirit
within them was producing rivers of living water enough for
themselves and others.

The deepening river – is that our spiritual experience?
Within the space of one and a half miles from its source,
Ezekiel's river was too deep to stand in. What does this picture
say to us? When our feet stand on a river bed we can feel safe,
secure, in control ... but when the depth of the water no longer
makes that possible it can be a frightening experience to trust
ourselves to the flow of the river.

But the river flowed from God's holy Temple down into a
very deep, dark place – the deadest place on earth, the Dead
Sea. The river was unstoppable. Was it Ezekiel 47 that inspired
John Newton to write

*Who can faint while such a river*
*Ever flows his thirst to assuage?*
*Grace which like the Lord, the Giver,*
*Never fails from age to age.*

"There is a river," the psalmist asserted in Psalm 46:4, AV
"the streams whereof shall make glad the city of God." So
marvellous is this river that wherever it flows everything lives.
All kinds of trees grow on both sides of the river and every
month they produce edible fruit. (Not once a year but 12 times
a year!) The leaves on the other hand provide healing for every
condition and ailment. When the river enters the Dead Sea –
where no life exists – the waters are healed and sweetened,
making it possible for fish to live and reproduce there so that
fishermen will spread their nets from Engedi to Eneglaim ...

and their catch will include many fish of every kind, just like the fishing possibilities of the Mediterranean Sea. But in the vicinity of the Dead Sea where the river does not reach, the marshes that remain will produce salt, necessary for the sustaining of life. This divine water means that no leaves on the trees wither, no crop of fruit fails for everything lives where the river goes (Ezek. 47:9).

The river of God ... from your innermost being shall flow rivers of living water. Ezekiel's vision is sent by God for you and me. "Son of man", says the angel to the prophet, "Have you seen this? Have you understood it?"

What is the secret of the flowing river? James Stewart comments, "Keep in the fellowship of Jesus. Keep going back to the manger, the Cross, the empty tomb. Stand with Peter on the shore, listening to His voice. Kneel with Mary Magdalene at His feet. Keep looking at Him, orientating your life to Him, identifying yourself with the will of God revealed in Him. His Spirit will do the rest."

Has the river stopped flowing? Are you in a marsh? Do you need to get back into the river? Late in his life, F.B. Meyer said, "I have prayed to God to keep the river of my life flowing. I don't want to end in a swamp!"

To students of the Bible, Ezekiel 47 always brings to mind the final chapter of the Bible, Revelation 22.

> Then he showed me a river of the water of life, clear as crystal, coming from the throne of God and of the Lamb, in the middle of its street. On either side of the river was the tree of life, bearing twelve kinds of fruit, yielding its fruit every month; and the leaves of the tree were for the healing of the nations. (Rev. 22:1–2, NASB)

It is doubly precious to have both the Old and New Testament declaring a similar truth.

So what is our response? Do we desire to get into the river and follow it wherever it flows? Do you really want it? Does the church want it? Are we crying out for the great rain?

In his recent book, *Streams of Living Water*, Richard Foster writes, "Today a mighty river is bursting forth ... it is a river of divine intimacy, a powerful river of holy living, a dancing river of jubilation in the Spirit, a broad river of unconditional love for all peoples. The astonishing new reality is this mighty flow brings together streams of life that have been isolated from one another for a very long time. No one models these dimensions of the spiritual life more fully than Jesus Christ. If we want to see this river of life in its most complete form, it is to Jesus we must turn."

Towards the end of the year 2000 I received a newsletter from a missionary friend. She had felt prompted to write out in full a vision that had been given to a modern Ezekiel by the name of Chad Taylor.

> I had a vision of a great river, like the one that was seen in Ezekiel 47. There stood men measuring and judging the depths of the river ... Then I saw many begin to build levees and dams to prevent flooding, frantically attempting to keep the river in its perimeters and banks ... Then I heard the voice of the Lord say, "It will defy every human effort ... it will flood the land."
>
> Suddenly in this vision, this river swelled beyond the confines of human configurations and swept the rocks and barriers away. A torrent of water began to fill the valleys and canyons, the dry deserted infertile places. In these very places the river now flooded and flowed. Then the voice of the Lord said, "In these deserted fields

overlooked by human reasoning is a great treasure. A pearl of great price. There in these places will a great harvest occur. In the forgotten places will an army now arise. They will be moved by this great river, they will be carried away into My Glory and Presence, only to emerge from its depths with a revelation, transfigured from the image of their previous selves, changed into My Image from glory to glory. No human effort to contain or corral this river will succeed. Only the ones that release it and *allow* it to flow where it must, will reap the benefits."

Then I beheld a wonder. In these deserted dry places suddenly gardens of abundance and fruitfulness sprang up. I saw millions working these fields of abundance with glory and joy. True harvest had visited the land. The river was flowing into every valley and crevice, filling the earth with the knowledge of the glory of God. Everywhere was the fruit of this river ... human lives redeemed and saved from the famine of religion and human reasoning. Unlike former revivals and awakening, this time the Spirit of the Lord refused to allow the river to be regulated and controlled.

"In this hour I will teach My church to flow with the river ... I will give them My heart and mind. They will be gatekeepers that *open* the gates that the King of Glory can come in. I will change the heart of Jonah in them that refuses to see the land changed and repent ..." In this vision I saw the great river of the present move of God turning. No longer was the church building at its headwaters, but rather the desert and the street were the mouth of this great river of revival. It was no longer dictated by human hands but by the hand of God. All restraint and hindrance was gone. A great army emerged

from its wake, alive and full of light and glory ... *the river of God had turned.*

Surely God continues to speak to us today, individually and corporately. May our ears hear and our hearts respond to the Holy Spirit's voice. For not only are prophets receiving visions but musicians are being given songs and poems such as Miriam Winter's "Psalm on Living Water":

*You are like a mountain spring O Fountain of Living Water;*
*I sip from the deep down freshness of your never-failing love.*
*You are like a summer rain O Sudden Benediction;*
*Drench my soul and quench my thirsting spirit with*
*     your peace.*
*You are like a raging sea, O Storm upon my Ocean;*
*Breaking to bits my fragile bark as I learn to lean on You.*
*You are like a waterfall Oasis in my Desert;*
*Source of my heart's survival in the press and stress of life.*
*You are like a cleansing flood, River of Reconciliation;*
*Washing away the selfish self-serving signs of my sinfulness.*
*You are like a bottomless well O Cup of Lifegiving Water;*
*Full up to overflowing. Praise be to you, O God.*[1]

A river has many moods and Miriam powerfully portrays this. In our lives we will inevitably experience God's river sometimes like dew to our dryness, sometimes like a storm to expose the flotsam within us.

The river is flowing. Are you experiencing its deepening flow? Do you have sufficient for your own life and is the overflow touching the lives of family, friends, neighbours, your church, your community, your nation?

May our prayer be, "River of God, flow over me. Penetrate

the deepest parts of my being. Cleanse and purify, renew and refresh, restore the joy of my salvation and recommission me for your service. Amen."

## Notes

1. Miriam Therese Winter, *Woman Word* (Medical Mission Sisters, 1990) p.III. Used with permission.

# TWENTY- FIRST CENTURY
# FREEDOM FOR WOMEN?

*Elaine Storkey*

# Biography

Elaine is Co-President of Tearfund, Vice-President of Cheltenham and Gloucester College and a member of the General Synod of the Church of England. She has lectured widely throughout the world, though many in the UK know her through her BBC broadcasts and regular *Thought for the Day* address on Radio 4. Elaine has spoken at several *Alive for God* events, bringing delegates her unique blend of social analysis and application of godly values to male–female relationships. Elaine has written extensively on the role of women and relationships: *What's Right with Feminism? The Search for Intimacy* (explores the barriers to good relationships): *Conversations in Christian Feminism* co-written with Margaret Hebblethwaite: and her latest publication *Men & Women Created or Constructed?* which looks at how men and women do, or do not differ.

Elaine was born in Wakefield, and is married to Alan Storkey, an economist, writer and lecturer. They have three sons.

In Britain, it often seems that many of the freedoms for which women campaigned long and hard in the 1970s have been fully realized. Women today enjoy considerably more benefits than either their mothers or grandmothers. On the whole they marry later, have fewer children, enjoy better health and stay younger longer. Many are in the kinds of jobs that make them financially independent. Women have access to all the professions and to the highest levels of education. At school, girls have been outstripping boys in exam performance for many years, and are being accepted into much-coveted vocational courses. Women own property, run their own businesses, have their own transport, make investments and can go into retirement with personal pensions. On the face of it, women have never had it so good; their lives have never been so unconstrained.

Yet this is only part of the picture. For in spite of all the apparent gains, there are some very negative aspects of life in the twenty-first century. Women struggle more with stress and depression than in previous decades, many more suffer from broken relationships, and an unprecedented number of women are bringing up children on their own. Divorce still leaves most women worse off financially than most men, and cohabitation means there is less stability in family relationships. This all means that for all the rise in living standards, many women are far from affluent. And, although we are told that exam performance and work skills give women self-confidence, there is also evidence that many women suffer acutely from low self-esteem. Eating disorders have never been as chronic or as widespread as they are now, and even very young girls are worrying about their body image. So, however much we applaud the changes that have taken place in the lives of women, it is not true that these have made life uniformly better.

## Raising the Key Questions

Many key secular women writers are now asking probing questions about what "equality" really means for women. Many of them believe that it is a misleading concept. Some women who analyse social change argue that we can easily be lulled into thinking that everything is solved in women's lives because we now have access to well-paid work. In a perceptive essay, one writer, Katherine Viner, doubts whether the progress has been anything like what people claim. For, she insists, there is much more to a woman's life than having a good job. And although there might be growing equality in the area of work, in more personal areas, many women are struggling. In particular, the stereotypes of what women should look like and how they should relate to men can be very oppressive. She writes:

> They might get equal pay, or they might be able to take their employer to a tribunal if they don't ... What they haven't got is the right for their body size to be unimportant, or the right, very often, to an equal sexual relationship.[1]

## Body-Image, Body-Hatred

We can see what she means when we look at the whole industry which has now developed around "body image". When we look at some statistics we could conclude that women in the UK in the twenty-first century are becoming obsessed by the way they look. There are now 65,000 operations of cosmetic surgery in Britain every year, the vast majority of which are performed on women. (Those who perform them, however, are overwhelmingly male – which is an interesting point to ponder.) Many of these operations are far from painless, and yet women subject themselves to the knife, bruises, scars, stitches and stretched skin, because they are taken in by the suggestion that without them they will look ugly. In fact, women in our country spend almost £9 billion on the beauty industry as a whole, in spite of the fact that consumer research reports regularly that little that is applied to the skin can actually keep the ageing process at bay. There is little doubt that all this indicates a high level of dissatisfaction among women about the way they look. Katherine Viner is concerned that plastic surgery has received such a high level of acceptance, especially when anorexia and self-abuse are becoming such problems. For her, these are all part of a bodily mutilation of women, and only a thin lines divides them.

> How can you defend a woman's right to liposuction but not her right to starve herself? Support her right to a boob job but deny her right to cut herself with razors? We are supposed to say that one form of mutilation is improvement, the other is harm, but the definition, when implants can leak and skin can go numb, are blurred. If it is self-hatred which makes women want to alter their body shape through anorexia and bulimia, should we not see plastic surgery ... in a similar critical light?[2]

What can be presented as freedom for women can be another form of bondage; bondage to a certain stereotype of what is an acceptable appearance. It is to be youthful, slim, well-toned, and well-contoured, even if we are approaching 70.

Those who have worked hard for women's freedom see this as bad news. In a passage that draws on biblical references, the veteran campaigner Germaine Greer laments the loss this can be, and questions what it does for women's deeper lives:

> Time and money spent tinkering with an old face and body are not available for other things, be they trips around the world or relieving the sufferings of the poor. To be so involved with the soul-case is the abomination of desolation, like a life spent in front of the mirror.[3]

## Saying "No" to Sex?

Along the same lines, the idea that the twenty-first century is one in which women now enjoy maximum sexual freedom is also being challenged. Some research has been done on what this actually means for women, especially young women. The report, "Sexual Behaviour and Attitudes in Britain", found that many young women who got involved in under-aged sex thought now that this had been "too early", and wished they had waited. Interestingly, most of these girls thought they had been "in love", whereas most of the boys clearly did not. Their motives were much more likely to be curiosity, or a desire to talk about it, or peer pressure from their friends.[4]

Many women writers are now suggesting that insisting women have equality because of work often hides deep inequality in intimate relationships. Those who have grown up in a permissive society see sexual activity as a normal part of their lives, with widespread contraception and the ease of obtaining an abortion having taken the anxiety out of sex. But has this really benefited young women, or given them a greater level of freedom and confidence in relationships? Germaine Greer doesn't think so. She spoke out at the Melbourne Book Festival, arguing that what really has happened is that women have lost the right to say "no". The current climate and atmosphere put more pressure on girls than ever before, and with the fear of unwanted pregnancies much reduced, they can be made to feel completely unreasonable if they object to having sex.

A study in the 1990s from the South Bank University on young people bore this out. The researcher, Janet Holland, a reader in sociology, reported her findings.

> Young women spoke of having unprotected sex, of not using condoms even when they were available, of making no protest at rape, of accepting violence, of coming under pressure to have unwanted intercourse.[5]

Other studies have documented a high level of non-consensual sex that was never reported to the police by girls, or even seen as anything wrong or abnormal. It is almost as if, in this era of sexual freedom, many young women are actually less ready to make a situation awkward by refusing the sexual attentions of someone they are dating.

## Mothers without Fathers

Britain has the highest cohabitation rate in Europe. Many women have come to accept that marriage is a thing of the past and that they have much more freedom in a relationship without legal ties. Little could be further from the truth. The figures on cohabiting relationships are not encouraging from a woman's point of view. For example, one survey found that men who were cohabiting were much more likely to be having sexual relationships with other women than men who were married. Then, the statistics suggest that women who are cohabiting when they conceive will be on their own with their child before it is two years old. Since the average cohabiting union lasts 32 months, this means that women increasingly have children with different men, and bring them up single-handed for a large part of their time. Effectively, what cohabitation means is that men are able to walk away from parenthood if they find it to be a limitation on their lifestyle, and the woman is often left in a very vulnerable position. If she does eventually marry, it may well be to a man who has no relation to any of her children.

Once again, this is hardly a description of freedom. Living off low pay, or social security benefits, having little adult company for much of the time, and often struggling with the task of being mother and father to small children can be demoralising and burdensome. Put against this aspect of some women's lives, all the gains in the workplace and education pale into insignificance.

## Time and Pressure

Finally, there is a level of pressure today that is greater than in almost any other society. Most women have not only one full-time job, but often two or three. Women with children often find they have hours of housework and child-care to organise as well as coping with their own careers. The resulting restlessness can be oppressive for women. Henri Nouwen puts his finger on something profoundly unsettling at the heart of society when he writes:

> While busy with and worried about many things, we seldom feel truly satisfied, at peace, at home. A gnawing sense of being unfulfilled underlies our filled lives. The great paradox is that many of us are busy and bored at the same time. While running from one event to the next, we wonder in our innermost selves if anything is really happening. While we can hardly keep up with our many

tasks and obligations, we are not so sure that it would make any difference if we did nothing at all. While people keep pushing us in all directions, we doubt if anyone really cares. In short, while our lives are full, we are unfulfilled.[6]

In many ways, there has always been restlessness in our culture. For true rest only comes for the human heart when it finds it in God. Yet there is something about life today that resists finding that rest, for we are all pushed by the demands of consumerism into thinking there must be material answers for all this. But ultimately, things fail to satisfy, and unless our relationships are themselves full of blessing, the task of living and going on can be a hollow experience.

## The Gospel for Women?

As Christian women, what are we to make of all this? Several things occur to me. The first is that we should acknowledge that we share the same concerns as those secular women who are making these observations. When people claim that women are now enjoying freedom, we want to know what this really means. Second is that we need to be sure that what Christianity has to say about women is enormously relevant for us today.

Very often, the church has focused its own attention on restrictions on women rather than on the freedom that we are given in the New Testament. In today's climate there is plenty of opportunity for correcting that. The culture of the first century was also difficult for women, with barriers and restrictions in almost every area of life. Yet Jesus broke through so many of those barriers to give women dignity and affirmation. The concern that Jesus showed to women went far beyond simple offers of "equality". He met them where they were and addressed their deepest needs. It was never a case of posturing or pretending. Jesus defended women against the harshness and hypocrisy of their culture then, and he does the same today. He shows that God's heart of love for women is far more liberating than anything that our twenty-first-century culture has to offer. We are important, not because of what job we do, or our youthfulness, or trim body size, or our marital state, or motherhood. We are important simply because we are made in God's image and are loved by God.

I believe we owe it to the women of the next generation not to lose our confidence in addressing the needs of women from a biblical point of view. Some of the key teachings that Christianity has always maintained about relationships can be seen as more relevant than ever in the climate of fragility and instability. It was Jesus who challenged the different standard of sexual morality when He stopped the crowd from stoning the woman taken in adultery. It was St Paul who urged that men should love their wives, and that involves being committed to them, encouraging them, sharing the upbringing of children. The gospel shows us what is freedom and what is not, and we should resist some of the misleading offers of our culture. We should also be grateful for those women outside the Church who see this too, and be prepared to learn from their insights. Who knows, if we forge a new relationship of listening to each other, many more might be ready to hear us when we share God's Good News for women.

For that Good News is as relevant today as it ever was: that God's love in Jesus Christ is real and effective; and when we experience that love for ourselves, we know what liberation means for women.

## Notes

1 Katherine Viner, "The Personal is Still Political" in Natasha Walter (ed.), *On the Move* (London: Virago, 1999), p. 25.

2 Ibid. p. 21.

3 Germaine Greer, *The Whole Woman* (London: Doubleday, 1999) p. 28.

4 K. Wellings, J. Field, A. Johnson and J. Wadworth, *Sexual Behaviour in Britain* (London: Penguin, 1995).

5 Janet Holland, *The Male in the Head: Young People, Heterosexuality and Power* (London: Tufnel Press, 1990).

6 Henri Nouwen, *Making All Things New: An Introduction to the Spiritual Life* (New York: Doubleday, 1981), pp. 23–4.

# CHAPTER EIGHT

# GIVE YOURSELF UP!

## Biography

An established secular and Christian journalist, Liz Trundle was editor of *Woman Alive* – the UK's only general interest consumer publication specifically for Christian women – until February 2003. Liz passionately believes that as a network of communication, *Woman Alive* events offer invaluable support, encouragement and guidance for Christian women in living out their faith on a daily basis. With Jeannette Barwick at Crusade for World Revival, Liz shared the vision to bring women together for a time of praise, celebration and teaching which resulted in the first national *Alive for God* tour in 1998.

Liz lives in West Sussex with her husband, St John and her two sons Jamie and Jack.

As editor of *Woman Alive* I have been involved in selecting and commissioning writers for *Inspiring Women*. Some contributors have asked for guidance on what to write and in each case I've encouraged them to "speak from the heart". Through the magazine I have learnt that nothing inspires other readers like a personal testimony of God's grace.

Now the shoe is firmly on the other foot and I can appreciate just how difficult it is to follow my own advice! How, I have pondered, could *my* story be the least bit inspiring to others? Faced with a severe attack of writer's block I resorted to my well-practised remedy of making a list. I jotted down my own key "life experiences" since becoming a Christian in 1994: separation, divorce, eating disorder, single parenthood, new job, new husband, new baby ... To my astonishment the synopsis revealed a packed eight years of change. I was humbled by what God had brought about in my life. And thankful that He had, in fact, given this opportunity for me to share my journey with others.

I have the privilege of reading people's accounts of God's intervention in their lives on a daily basis. Women from all walks of life and situations write to me at *Woman Alive*. But their stories invariably share a common theme: they show how the Lord has brought them to a point of surrender to His will. It seems that one of the hardest things for Christian women to do today is to let God take full control.

The demands on our time and energy have turned us into a generation of multi-taskers. Our daily lives require an overwhelming amount of control to meet the demands of work

and family – to keep all our juggling balls in the air. But as we conform to worldly expectations, it is often difficult to decipher God's voice of direction and authority. This chapter is a personal record of my journey from fanatical control and self-sufficiency, to resting in God's will and destiny for my life. The journey is by no means over – God still has a lifetime of teaching for me – and He will not guide anyone else in quite the way He has guided me. But I offer it as a source of encouragement for all those struggling to keep chaotic and stressful lives under control.

## Happy-go-lucky

Looking back 20 years, I remember feeling that I had life fairly well sorted out! I had given up my job as a journalist in the UK, rented out my flat in Brighton and gone on a world trip with my future husband. We shared professions and aspirations and the desire to live and work abroad. We wanted to be free to experience new lifestyles and cultures. I interpreted this freedom as true fulfilment and I perceived no need for God in my life.

My boyfriend and I were not, of course, unusual in living under this illusion. Most people in our godless society today do. So how did God break through this independent exterior so that I became responsive to the gospel? Was I just more gullible than my friends and relatives? No – my journey began with prayer, a fact that I was oblivious to at the time. People were praying for me and the strength of those prayers proved more powerful than the bondage of self-sufficiency. "The prayer of a righteous man is powerful and effective" (James 5:16). Keep on praying for those you love!

Our travelling days took us to the Far East and Hong Kong where we settled down, and eventually got married and had a baby boy. It was at this point that God chose to introduce me to several Christians in the Territory. I met co-workers of the renowned missionary Jackie Pullinger, and my closest friend during those early years of parenthood was responsible for setting up the Hong Kong section of the prayer network Women Aglow. While I found their total dependency on Jesus and the Bible off-putting at this stage, their confidence in life and peace of mind was attractive. I secretly wished myself among them.

As for myself, I was rapidly losing weight and had become controlled by unhealthy eating "rituals" and a strict diet. When our son was nearly four years old we decided to return to England so he could grow up in contact with his grandparents and cousins. On our return I met an old friend who had tried to convert me to Christianity before my travelling days. I had been completely disinterested, but now, with the happy-go-lucky days of my twenties a distant memory, I was keen to know more. How could Jesus offer "answers" to my troubled mind and obsessive behaviour?

My friend encouraged me to go to church, so I began attending a New Frontiers International church in Brighton, and I read the Bible and introductory books to Christianity. I learnt more of how Jesus offers peace and salvation, and a "way out" of perpetual sin and habitual behaviour. My mind was convinced and shortly afterwards, with the help and encouragement of church members, I asked Jesus to touch my spirit and bring that radiating peace into my heart. From then on there was no turning back. I was raring to go for the Lord!

Having given my life to Jesus I felt at last that I was moving in the right direction. However, I was reluctant to relinquish total control to God; to a certain extent I was fearful of what might happen if I did. There was a sense of security in my old

familiar ways. I clung to that "comfort zone".

Fortunately God is more concerned with our condition than our comfort! He was not interested in pampering to my superficial objections. Instead He has slowly and steadfastly helped me to hand over the reins of my life to Him. I had to admit to God, and to myself, that I had become addicted to a rigid eating pattern that was a form of bondage – a habit or state that God doesn't intend us to bear. Speaking out my feelings to God in prayer gave me the courage to be open and honest with myself and those around me, and to seek professional help.

Recovery has been punctuated by several relapses and has taken years rather than months. But knowing that I could not be totally free through my own effort and that I was in *God's hands*, I did not give up hope. For me this is how Jesus has shown His strength through my human weakness. I can say with confidence that with Him there is an answer.

With such positive changes in my life, I expected my husband to notice the difference in me and instantly want the same for himself. I fully believed that within a few weeks of my conversion he would be eagerly accompanying me to church. Meanwhile, aware that I was a strong-willed person who invariably wanted the last word, I worked hard on "humbling myself". I consciously took more of a back seat in our marriage and allowed my husband the freedom to steer domestic decisions. After all, I surmised, wasn't that the model of a "biblical" wife as depicted in Proverbs 31?

To my frustration, my husband barely noticed any difference! He was pleased that I had found fulfilment but certainly didn't see his own salvation through Jesus. Instead he sought inner peace and confidence through relaxation techniques and self-improvement classes. With growing disillusionment I sought solace in God's Word and clung to Paul's encouraging words in Romans: "Be joyful in hope, patient in affliction, faithful in prayer" (Rom. 12:12).

God did answer my prayers but certainly not in the way I expected. My husband's immediate conversion was not part of God's master plan. I couldn't speed his salvation along by becoming a domestic goddess! As with my eating disorder, God wanted me to give up control and release my husband's future to Him. At the same time He offered me the opportunity to strengthen my own faith through the editorship of *Woman Alive*.

Elation at achieving my long-held ambition of editing a magazine, and being able to apply my faith to my work, was mixed with feelings of total inadequacy and inexperience to do the job. But God was clearly steering my path and I found a "supernatural" confidence in the knowledge that I could trust Him if not myself! I had also learnt a valuable lesson of faith: that God treats us all as individuals and that my husband's conversion was not my worry or responsibility. God is concerned about our present spiritual development. All we have to do is to cooperate with His plan. "My sheep listen to my voice; I know them, and they follow me. I give them eternal life, and they shall never perish" (John 10:27–28).

## Fighting for Love

Despite the UK's escalating divorce rate and the consequent increase of divorcees in our church congregations, divorce remains a taboo subject in Christian circles. Recently *Woman Alive* ran an article entitled "Marriage Mistakes". In it Christian women told of their experiences of unsuccessful relationships and marriage breakdown. The feature was followed by an outcry in our postbag! Many readers felt that

these women, by sharing their stories, were encouraging others to abandon their marriages as soon as the going gets tough.

This, of course, was not the intention of the article. The aim was to empathise with women who were currently struggling in difficult marriages and to offer a message of hope: that God can redeem all situations, including bad marriages. Their experiences showed how sometimes God works for good within a marriage, and at other times He offers a way out from a marriage decision made independently of Him.

Shortly after taking on the editorship of *Woman Alive*, my own marriage reached a crisis point. My attempts at being the ideal "biblical" wife had completely failed to improve my relationship with my husband or bring us closer together. At this point I consciously handed my marriage over to God in prayer.

Within two months my husband made the decision not to move with me and our son to our long-awaited family home along the coast. His "declaration" left me in an emotional whirlwind; shock, fear and anxiety were mixed with relief that God was clearly beginning to direct the future path of my marriage. Meanwhile I began the process of grieving a failed marriage, and moving on – physically to a new home and emotionally as a lone parent. At first I viewed our separation as a short-term "break". But as the months went by my husband made it clear that he considered the separation to be permanent.

I do not regret the time I spent with my ex-husband. Along with many shared experiences the marriage brought us a bright and healthy son. But I do accept that God had a "higher" plan for my life; a plan that embraced both divorce and single parenthood. I felt more than ever that my future was now in

His hands. "Find rest, O my soul, in God alone; my hope comes from him. He alone is my rock and my salvation" (Psa. 62:5–6).

The following five years proved to be a time of personal spiritual growth, and significant development for *Woman Alive* as a magazine. I missed adult company at home, but felt it a privilege to be able to focus fully on my work, and bring up my son in a Christian environment. God has blessed the magazine with a team of top Christian writers and a grateful and growing readership.

## The Battle for My Mind

I have been aware, however, of the efforts of the "evil one" to undermine this progress. As God is glorified the devil picks up speed, employing subtle methods of deceit and discouragement. He wants us back in our "comfort zone" where our usefulness to God is inhibited and restricted. A common tactic is to engender feelings of guilt, which hold us back; guilt at following God's plan "at the expense" of worldly expectations. Alternatively, conscious of the sin in our lives, we feel too unworthy to be used by the Lord.

The Holy Spirit is like a strong flowing current, moving in God's direction. As Christians, we all long to relinquish control and plunge unhindered into the flow of the Spirit. But people are pleading with us from the "safety" of the shore: "I need you!" "Don't rock the boat". And a voice within you says that it's impossible to stay afloat because you are weighed down by sin. God wants us to turn away from these pleas and to respond fully to the Holy Spirit.

As my life began to turn around – following the break-up of my marriage, and taking on the editorship of *Woman Alive* – I was conscious that my eating disorder still exercised a hold

 CHAPTER EIGHT

over my life. For me this was my source of destructive guilt. Although I was a normal weight, and no longer tied to a strict daily eating ritual, I still experienced feelings of guilt. I felt guilty if I under-ate as I knew people would disapprove. And I felt twice as guilty if I over-ate as this usually meant a night-time binge of "bad food" like biscuits and bars of chocolate. The following morning I would be filled with regret, guilt and self-loathing. I would feel "paralysed" in my work for God until I had returned to at least some sort of sensible eating plan.

As I have described, I had wrestled with this unhealthy relationship with food for years, and I was weighed down by the guilt. But God had brought me this far and I knew that I could trust Him to help me through stages of weakness. I also knew that I had to be proactive in fighting it. When I felt defeated, instead of devising ways of making my body feel "clean" from the food I'd eaten, I determined to open my Bible and read God's Word. I prayed for a balanced approach to eating and consciously *rejected* feelings of guilt associated with over- and under-eating.

I found that as I practised *not feeling guilty*, guilt began to affect me less and less. I was able to flow in God's Spirit regardless of how "well" I'd eaten that day. I became more receptive to His will, and His will alone. Most importantly where guilt had previously dictated my action, God's will was now my driving force. I was learning to hand over more control of my life to Him.

If you glimpse just a small part of yourself through this account of my journey so far, I pray that you will join me too in submitting to God's refining and healing process. It is a priceless freedom worth fighting for. It is a freedom that will allow you to throw off the bondage of control and to give God the care of everything. And truly I write this from my heart.

# CHAPTER NINE

## YOUR WORD IS A LAMP

*Wendy E. Vijo.*

# Biography

Wendy Virgo became a Christian as a little girl of seven. Brought up in a missionary-minded home, she thought that probably her life would be spent overseas. However, she met and married Terry Virgo, who, it seemed was destined to pastor in a small English church! Any aspirations to go abroad had to be put on hold. But they found they could not be content with the status quo. God put in them a passion to see the church renewed and restored. Through many heartaches, they gradually saw a beautiful community of Spirit-filled Christians arise. Requests for help came from other groups, and eventually new churches began to spring up. In the midst of all this, Wendy had five children – which provided plenty of opportunities to grow in faith and patience! She also developed a love for the Bible and faith in its relevance for women today, and her own teaching ministry grew.

In the mid 1980s the network of churches Wendy and Terry were working with was named New Frontiers. New Frontiers now has churches in 24 nations, and contacts in many others.

Wendy now finds herself in the exciting position of travelling frequently to many nations alongside Terry. She enjoys opportunities not only to teach but to befriend other leaders' wives, to pray, prophesy and generally to seek to be involved in the advance of the Kingdom of God.

I was walking along Victoria Street in my lunch hour when I saw the dress. It was dark blue with white dots, and lace around the neck line and edges of the sleeves. To my naïve eyes it looked elegant and sophisticated. I was on a shoestring budget but the July sale had brought it down to an affordable price, so I bought it, thinking it would bring a much needed touch of class to my extremely meagre wardrobe.

In a month's time I was going to get married and be a pastor's wife. I had absolutely no idea what that would entail, and the dress in a way personified my ignorance. I suppose I had a vague idea that being a pastor's wife would require standing around at various functions looking decorative! In fact that never happened. I am not sure if the dress was ever worn. Not only did the need to look decorative rarely arise but five pregnancies meant that my figure ballooned and shrank with amazing regularity; and eventually the dress was consigned to the outer darkness of Oxfam.

Actually, I had never wanted to be a pastor's wife. That was much too tame! I wanted to do something adventurous, to be a pioneer, to be radical.

*Just as I am, young, strong and free,*
*To be the best that I can be ...*

These lines summed up my hopes and aspirations as I sang them enthusiastically, and others like them, in my childhood years. I first heard God speak to me in a Crusader class when I was seven years old. As I handed over my young life to Him, I was flooded with joy and the knowledge of His love for me.

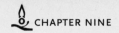 

I knew then that my life was not my own and that I must find out what God wanted me to do with it.

So began the search for destiny. It had to be something heroic! I always had my nose stuck in a book, and many were the novels, romances and biographies that I devoured. But increasingly my taste grew toward biography and the stories of pioneer missionaries enthralled me. I read of Hudson Taylor going to China, of intrepid women such as Francesca and Evangeline French and Mildred Cable, trekking into the Gobi deserts of Outer Mongolia, the first white women ever seen in those remote areas. I read of Mary Slessor in West Africa, Amy Carmichael in Southern India, Isobel Kuhn in the tribal mountains of Laos. My young heart yearned to be crossing impassable rivers, toiling up the foothills of the Himalayas, or at least swaying across the Sahara on a camel!

Coming from a family rich with missionary interest, I had many opportunities to meet missionaries. My mother was on the candidates committee of the Overseas Missionary Fellowship and so we often had missionaries to stay in our home. Many became greatly loved friends. I remember one asking me one day, just as I was going through the front door, if I was going to be a missionary. I was slightly affronted by her question. "I might be," I replied, my offhand manner concealing the inner excitement that it provoked.

The idea stayed lurking in my heart through my growing years. But another question persisted in the forefront of my mind. I might end up on the mission field eventually, but what was I going to do in the meantime? I knew that you could not just present yourself to a country as a missionary and be received with open arms. You had to train as something first, and then go to that mysterious place, the "Mission Field". This was a phrase often heard in our house, and was spoken of as if it were a geographical place rather than a concept. As a child, I pictured it as a vast green field, dotted with white girl-guide tents, from which missionaries sallied forth with large bundles of tracts to evangelise neighbouring villages. It was some time before I understood the connection with the verse in the Gospels where the Lord Jesus exhorted His disciples to pray for labourers to be sent to reap in fields ready for harvest.

I spent much of my last two years in school in debate with my scripture teacher who taught the Bible from a liberal point of view and poured doubt on its veracity and authenticity. The more I argued with her, the more convinced I became of the truth it contained. I was required to study large chunks of it for one of my A-level courses, and I remember one evening in particular as I was reading Romans 5 how God's love poured down on me afresh as I read that "God demonstrates his love for us in that while we were still sinners, Christ died for us."

How wonderful it would be, I thought, to have teachers in schools who not only taught the Bible, but believed it! What about me? I could do it! After all, here I was, "young, strong and free ..." Look out all you modernists, here I come on my white charger, plunging into the field of education, to bring divine wisdom! I would have a great career in education, and then sacrifice it all by heroically disappearing to the mission field to do mighty exploits for God.

It seemed a good idea to do a theological degree at a college where the Bible was believed in and respected, so I applied to London Bible College, and was accepted. My first year was a "breaking out of home and adolescence" sort of year. But at the beginning of my second year, God spoke to me very clearly. "Seek God for Himself." What a novel idea! I had sought God for forgiveness, guidance, love, but not for Himself alone. I was deeply stirred. How wonderful it would be to know God

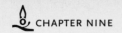

closely, and not just to have "quiet times" because that was what a Christian was expected to do.

I embarked on a journey of discovery, and something extraordinary began to happen. I found that I was pursuing God with a growing hunger. As my appetite sharpened, lectures, meals, hockey matches, all became an interruption in the pursuit of God. There must be more, I thought.

A controversial topic among the students at that time – 1966 – was the baptism in the Holy Spirit. It had never been referred to in my Brethren Assembly; but as I prayed, read current books, and listened to testimonies from the few students who claimed to have entered into this experience, I became convinced that this was what I needed.

That summer, I was on an evangelistic team in Sussex led by Terry Virgo. One afternoon in Littlehampton, the team was scheduled to take an open-air meeting on the beach, but torrential rain poured down. The rest of the team sensibly stayed away, leaving Terry and me standing in a church porch, looking forlornly at the downpour. "Why don't we go in, and I could show you in the Bible the teaching on the baptism in the Spirit?" Terry suggested.

That afternoon was a turning point in my life as Terry unfolded to me the coming of the Spirit in the Book of Acts. He then went to John 7 where Jesus gave an invitation to those who were thirsty to come to him and drink. "And this he said of the Spirit ..." He turned to Luke 11, which speaks of the Father's eagerness to give the Holy Spirit to those who ask. The penny dropped; faith had been inspired by the Word of God. Later on that night I asked my room-mate to pray for me. The Holy Spirit fell on me, and I spoke in tongues for most of the night! How my thirsty soul drank of Him! How I rejoiced in His love; and how I must have alarmed my friends and relations as I rushed around telling them of this new discovery!

I still planned to become a teacher, but had to admit to myself that my call to the mission field had not yet materialised. My upbringing had taught me that every missionary had to have a "call". To tell the truth I had no deep feelings about anywhere in particular. I tried to drum up a call to the Middle East, but it fizzled out. I nearly got as far as Belgium once, but again, it never got off the ground.

One of my friends had gone to Malawi for a year with the Voluntary Services Overseas programme. Perhaps if I tried that route, I would get a call while I was there. I filled in application forms and came to the space left for a reference. Casually, I thought my tutor would do it in a jiffy. But I knew she would ask me if I had prayed about this; so before I rushed out of the room to ask her, I dropped on my knees by the bed and asked God for guidance. I picked up my Bible and opened it at Psalm 32:9: "Be not like the horse or mule which have no understanding ..." Oh no! God was speaking to me about not charging off undirected and unbridled like a wild horse! Another door seemed to shut in my face! I was frustrated.

All this time I had resolutely resisted attempts by members of the opposite sex to engage my affections. Having had a few unfortunate entanglements in the past, I now regarded any liaison as a dangerous distraction from finding the will of God. As it says in Matthew 6, "If the eye is single, the whole body will be full of light." I wanted to be single-eyed, and if that meant being single as in "unmarried", I was willing. I told the Lord that I would quite like to be married but I really wanted to serve Him with a whole heart, and I could not see that it was possible to do both.

For some months now, Terry Virgo had been showing a tentative interest. I tried to distance myself from him but, strangely, he kept unexpectedly showing up. I began to acknowledge that in all my daydreams about doing exploits for God, I could picture myself conducting a lively correspondence with him from the depths of a jungle or half way up a mountain. Of course, I would be doing something heroic, but he would probably be buried in a boring little church somewhere in England! When his overtures became persistently obvious, I spelt it out. I could not respond because I was looking for God's will.

Terry was very patient. About six months later, I woke up to the fact that to marry him was, in fact, God's will for my life! This amazed me, but I was deliriously happy about it. What a discovery! After all my daydreams, suddenly it seemed I was destined to be a pastor's wife!

Pastors' wives had not figured in my life up to now. I had been raised in a Christian family which belonged to an evangelical group known as the Brethren, who preached the gospel every Sunday at 6.30, and on Sunday mornings gathered, literally, around the Lord's Table. The seating was arranged with a table in the centre on which was placed the bread and wine. There was no set ministry; any (man) could bring a hymn, reading, prayer or message. (The women had to be quiet and wear hats!) Given that all believers had equal access to God, there was thought to be no need of an ordained or recognised minister. As there were no pastors, there were therefore no pastors' wives.

My experience was therefore nil, but I viewed the prospect cheerfully. Everything would be fine. We were in love and God was with us! What could go wrong? After our wedding, we began life together in the little town of Seaford in Sussex. Terry had been invited to be the pastor of a small group, an embryonic church, which soon began to grow.

The next years were formative to our whole understanding of church planting, growth and government. They were painful, frustrating but also exciting years. From the start, I felt like a little ship embarking on uncharted waters. I longed for a mentor, another leader's wife on whom I could model, but found none. This was because we were in a fairly unique position in those days. Terry and I had both come from solid evangelical backgrounds, but knew that our experience of church life was difficult for new believers to break into. Now we were in a small evangelical free church, seeking to implement principles to build a church full of the vibrant life of the Spirit that we saw in the New Testament. This often involved radical change and painful readjustment, and a tenacious hold on the vision that God had given us. I did not know anyone else who was seeking to do this at the time.

Sometimes I felt I was barely keeping my head above water. I was grappling with the new experiences of being a wife and mother (which were not boring, but were very exhausting), as well as seeking to stand loyally by Terry who was being pulverised by the pressures of bringing charismatic life into a church that was, on the whole, content with the status quo. This was one of my hardest lessons: to have to stand by and watch my husband being criticised and withstood, by those who were uncomprehending about what God could do with a company of people who were willing to take risks and strike out into new territory with Him.

Sometimes I would hear him come in from yet another abortive, tense elders' meeting and go straight upstairs to the bedroom. I would find him face down on the carpet in an agony of frustration, praying his way back to faith in the vision.

Anger and resentment would rise in my heart. "It isn't fair!" I raged inwardly. "They don't know how much he pours himself out for them and how he is only trying to be obedient to God!" Then I had to learn to get my own attitude right. I learned that if you are trying to teach a church to worship in a style consistent with the New Testament, where the believers are instructed to come together ready to participate, you have to come with a clean heart. You cannot teach them, "Be filled with the Spirit, speaking to one another in psalms and hymns and spiritual songs, singing and making melody in your heart to the Lord, always giving thanks in all things ..." if your own heart is so polluted that there is a wall between you and your brothers and sisters.

There was one lively lady in the church that I often crossed swords with. We clashed. Looking back, I can see now that probably a lot of it was immaturity on my part. But one night I could stand it no longer. Terry went to bed, while I determined to pray it through. For some reason I wrote down all the things I detested about this lady. As I was looking at the list, I was devastated to hear the Lord say, "You have just written down a picture of yourself." I was totally undone, and wept my way through repentance. The scripture about trying to remove a speck from someone's eye when you have a plank sticking out of your own became humblingly real. Slowly we rebuilt our relationship, and eventually became firm friends.

One by one we prayed people into the baptism of the Holy Spirit. This immediately brought a number of issues to the surface; for instance, these people newly filled with the Spirit were eager to start using spiritual gifts. But when and how? How were they to be regulated? Who had the authority? The elders? But they were not altogether happy with what was going on! The church was growing rapidly, worship was lively, full of the presence of God; gifts of prophecy, tongues and interpretation were flowing; but there were tensions and conflicts in the heart of the church. One day in despair, Terry wrote out a letter of resignation. It was beautifully worded and argued, but as we looked at each other, we knew God had not told him to run away. Slowly, he tore it up. Through it all, I watched God putting steel into my lovely, easy-going husband. He lost none of his tender-heartedness, he still hated conflict, but I saw him grow strong in faith as he put God's requirements first.

But I still longed for an older woman to help me. One day I cried out to God, "Show me someone who has trodden this path before. I make so many mistakes!"

The Lord spoke clearly. "I will teach you from leaders' wives in the Bible. Learn from them."

I was excited! I began to study the Scriptures with a new zeal, searching out the wives of leaders with a new sense of identification. I found that they were human beings who made mistakes and sometimes had wrong attitudes. There was David's first wife, Michal, a tragic figure who allowed the suffocation of rejection to shape her attitude to herself, to others, and eventually to God himself. She ended up lonely and barren. Then there was Job's wife, who had no depth of character or relationship with God, but relied on her husband's faith; so when the cold winds of tragedy blew, she had no resources, no way to receive comfort or to give it. "Curse God and die!" she screamed at Job.

But what about Esther? Ah, there was a goldmine! She was a misfit, an alien, a nobody. But through humility, obedience and judicious use of what natural resources she had – in her case a beautiful face – she caught the attention of the king. But she did not stop at finding a cushy place for herself in the sun, ignoring the plight of her compatriots. When a massacre threatened, she prayed and fasted and courageously but humbly confronted the king. Everything was turned around in a miraculous way and she ended up with ruling authority, wearing the king's signet ring. What a model! I loved it.

Eve was a never-ending source of instruction. I avidly pored over the first few chapters of Genesis, meditating on her amazing origin, her name, her relationship with Adam, and the vast influence she had on him. Scary! But I also discovered that she was his helper. As I explored that word, it opened up a new perspective to me in my own role as helper to my husband. In our day, we have pushed the concept of "helper" into a derogatory category. In Western vocabulary, it is perceived as secondary, inferior, a sort of appendage. But I was awestruck to realise that God Himself is our model; He is our "Help and Shield", and the Holy Spirit is also sent to be our "Helper". That put a new and glorious construction on my role as a helper, elevating it to something modelled by God Himself. Not so inferior after all!

Deborah, Naomi, Rebekah, even Samson's fickle Delilah: I learned lessons from them all. As time went on I found great delight in sharing what I was learning with other women. Requests to speak at various gatherings followed. By this time we had planted other churches and begun to work overseas. I found that women in countries all over the world basically have the same needs, desires and problems, but in different cultural contexts. I have become convinced that there is no problem which is too complex, difficult or "modern" for which the Bible has no wisdom.

I am no longer a pastor's wife; my husband has an overseeing role to hundreds of churches in many nations. But in every church in every country we feel secure teaching principles that are tried and tested in the Word of God. The Bible is a powerful weapon, exposing the condition of the human heart and giving guidelines for building secure lives. It is relevant and trustworthy today, and we dilute it, disregard it or tamper with it at our peril.

CHAPTER TEN

# TAKING OFF THE MASK

Helena Wilkinson

# Biography

After working as a research assistant in the psychiatric department of a Zulu hospital, Helena trained in counselling. For four years she edited *Carer and Counsellor* and worked for Crusade for World Revival (CWR) in the editorial and counselling departments. She is the author of six books, including *Puppet on a String*, her account of anorexia, and *Beyond Chaotic Eating*, a Christian approach to eating disorders. Helena is founder of the Kainos Trust, a Christian charity that supports people with eating disorders through counselling, residential courses, teaching and drop-in days and correspondence. Helena speaks regularly on eating disorders and related subjects and was recently described as "probably the best eating-disorders counsellor in Europe". Convinced of Jesus' power to heal, Helena speaks with direction and sensitivity.

"What is REAL?" asked the Rabbit one day, when they were lying side by side near the nursery fender, before Nana came to tidy the room. "Does it mean having things that buzz inside you and a stick-out handle?"

"Real isn't how you are made," said the Skin Horse. "It's a thing that happens to you. When a child loves you for a long, long time, not just to play with, but REALLY loves you, then you become Real."

"Does it hurt?" asked the Rabbit.

"Sometimes," said the Skin Horse, for he was always truthful. "When you are Real you don't mind being hurt."

"Does it happen all at once, like being wound up," he asked, "or bit by bit?"

"It doesn't happen all at once," said the Skin Horse. "You become. It takes a long time. That's why it doesn't often happen to people who break easily, or have sharp edges, or who have to be carefully kept. Generally, by the time you are Real, most of your hair has been loved off, and your eyes drop out and you get loose in the joints and very shabby. But these things don't matter at all, because once you are Real you can't be ugly, except to people who don't understand."[1]

*The Velveteen Rabbit* is a beautiful story that illustrates the value of being real – of taking off the mask, daring to show ourselves warts and all, and being loved and accepted for who we are, even at the risk of being rejected. The story shows that it takes both time and courage to reach the point of being real and that by the time you do reach this point you have gone through many different life experiences.

Becoming real is very rewarding and creates a depth to our relating. So what stops us from taking steps towards achieving this? Two things: our pain and our defences.

Just as most plants need water and light to survive so we need to receive consistent love in order to become mature and emotionally healthy adults. For many people that love process has been interrupted, often at quite an early age, and feelings of insecurity, low self-worth, and insignificance emerge. The hurting inner self feels more open to criticism, attack and rejection from others; and defences start to be built before we realise. We begin to wear a mask that covers up the real person and only lets others see aspects of ourselves. We fear that in exposing our true selves we may be hurt, let down or seen not to be good enough.

Rather than feel our pain and deal with it we devise strategies, wear masks and develop patterns of behaviour that take the focus off our hurts and our feelings of unworthiness. These masks and patterns often serve well in shifting the focus, but because they are not legitimate they can never meet our need for love and worth, and so never enable us to become real or free. Instead we become slaves to a set of rules and to "oughts", "shoulds" and "musts".

In my work as Director of Kainos Trust for eating disorders, I see people wearing many different masks, giving out messages such as: "I'm OK, I don't need anyone"; "I never get angry, I just want to please you"; "I'll talk about anything, except what matters to me"; the list could go on and on. They develop patterns around food, weight and relating in attempts to feel in control. These coping mechanisms have often been brought into operation as a result of severe trauma, lack of confidence, low self-worth and deep unhappiness. Sexual abuse and bullying are two main factors behind eating disorders.

Most therapists and doctors do not believe that people who have learned to manage their pain, fears and uncomfortable feelings about themselves through addictive and self-destructive patterns can ever make a full recovery. Instead they feel that people can only learn to cope with the eating disorder or maintain degrees of freedom unless under stress, when it is more than likely to return.

At Kainos we believe, and have been witness to the fact, that people can and do fully recover. If the underlying issues are dealt with sufficiently and people learn new, healthy ways of coping, and they learn to be real and not wear a mask, then the eating disorder ceases to serve a purpose. The following true story is an example of how pain in childhood led to the developing of a coping mechanism and the wearing of a mask but, more importantly, how over a period of time the mask came off and freedom and healing came about.

Jo had extremely low self-worth and had suffered from anorexia from the age of 12. She had learnt to wear a mask that covered up any signs of weakness and neediness and gave out a message that said: "I don't need anyone and I deserve nothing."

Looking back, she says:

> I now realise that a number of factors contributed to my becoming anorexic, including bullying, low self-esteem, a fear of puberty and my unrealistic perfectionism. I spent a month and a half in a general hospital being tube-fed before being transferred to an adolescent unit, where I spent two and a half of the next four years. I was violent, hated everyone, and couldn't bring myself to eat anything.

I applied to do medicine at university and secured a place but I deferred my entry for a year. It was during this time that I became a Christian. Despite believing in Jesus I was still depending on my weight, eating and exercise for my worth and security, and anything that interrupted my plans for these made me feel completely out of control. I began at medical school and got through the first year, living on the edge. However, the medical school decided that I was too ill to continue studying and said that I had to withdraw until my condition improved. I was absolutely devastated as my studies had been the one thing keeping me going, giving me some sense of purpose, and now even that had been taken away. I felt a complete failure and worth nothing.

Consequently my condition worsened and I had to have a major operation to save my toes, which I was about to lose as severe chilblains had turned gangrenous. I was getting frequent blackouts, and felt on the verge of death. Several nights I dreamt that I had died and was surprised to find myself alive the next morning. This was the worst time – knowing I had to face yet another day feeling frozen to the bone, and being unceasingly tormented and driven by anorexic rules and thoughts. I couldn't let myself eat anything until I had reached a state of complete emptiness when my body was literally crying out for food.

When things could get no worse and I could feel no lower I went on a Kainos residential course for anorexics and bulimics, not really knowing what anyone there could say or do that numerous counsellors and psychiatrists I had seen in the past had not said already. I hadn't reckoned on God's power!

Through Helena's teaching that week I was suddenly able to *feel* what I had previously *known* in my head – that God loved *me*. I am valuable because I am God's child. I used to believe that others were valuable, but could not seem to apply this to myself. I immediately felt so secure and suddenly felt I no longer needed to get my feelings of worth from starvation and exercise. My identity was in Jesus, and I just didn't need or want the anorexia any more.

Jo had let her mask down; she had let God and others into her vulnerability because she knew, without any doubt, that she was loved. She went on to gain weight, to grow in her feelings of worth and confidence; and she has since returned to medical school.

Jo is one of lots of people I could tell you about who have moved from a place of hiding, covering up, wearing a mask and trying to cope through taking control over food and weight, to a place of becoming real. For each of these people several things made the difference and enabled them to reach that place – the unconditional love of God, the knowledge of His love for them, bonding with others and having a sense of purpose in life.

In our state of vulnerability we need to turn to God as our rock and our place of safety. We need to know Him as the Good Shepherd, who is trustworthy, who guides and who protects. Perhaps the most well-known biblical passage to help us to do this is Psalm 23.

Psalm 23 is powerful because it creates an image that makes sense to us, but to understand that image properly we need to look at the psalm in the time and culture in which it was written. In twenty-first-century Britain, most of us have little concept of what a shepherd does. In biblical times a shepherd was very important. The Hebrew word for shepherd comes from the words *Ro'eh* (roe aye), which is related to neighbour, friend; and *Re'ah* (ray arh), which shows love and community, nurturing and feeding. Out of this second word comes the Latin word *pastor* – to look after.

If we are going to allow God to heal our hurts and bring down our defences we need to look at Psalm 23 through the eyes of a shepherd, and we need to reset the context. When they read about sheep in the Bible, many people think in terms of English sheep and pastures – rolling hills, lush green grass and a picture of peace and tranquillity. We may wonder, in that context, quite why a shepherd is needed – the sheep seem to take care of themselves most of the day!

However, in biblical times the picture couldn't be more different. The Hebrew word used in Psalm 23 for where the sheep were located is *mid-bar*, translated "desert" or "wilderness". It wouldn't have been a lush green area, but a dry place with little or no rainfall – no good for crops but fine for grazing. Where the sheep themselves were grazing would have been an arid area, even if close to a more fertile area.

We can't understand the beauty of Psalm 23, and the vital role of the shepherd, unless we understand the wilderness. Imagine a dry, dusty, hot place where there seems so little life; where one sheep being separated from the group would have put that sheep's life in danger and where mere existence would have, at times, been hard work. Perhaps it sounds familiar? Our lives can be like that – we can feel dry, desolate, empty, isolated and surrounded by nothing. The more we can picture and feel the desolation of the wilderness, the more we can see how powerful the words of Psalm 23 are:

The Lord is my shepherd,
I shall not want.
He makes me lie down in green pastures;
He leads me beside quiet waters.
He restores my soul;
He guides me in the paths of righteousness
For His name's sake. (Psalm 23:1–3, NASB)

When we understand how arid the wilderness is, we appreciate all the more in the psalm how life-restoring those green pastures are.

Isaiah 35 describes the wilderness, but in the middle of the passage is another word, *ara-bah*, which speaks of the blossom that springs up in the arid area.

The wilderness and the desert will be glad,
And the Arabah will rejoice and blossom;
   like the crocus
It will blossom profusely
And rejoice with rejoicing and shout for joy.
The glory of Lebanon will be given to it,
The majesty of Carmel and Sharon.
They will see the glory of the Lord,
The majesty of our God.
Encourage the exhausted and
   strengthen the feeble.
Say to those with anxious heart,
"Take courage, fear not.
Behold, your God will come with vengeance;
The recompense of God will come,
But he will save you."
Then the eyes of the blind will be opened,

And the ears of the deaf will be unstopped.
Then the lame will leap like a deer,
And the tongue of the dumb will shout for joy.
For waters will break forth in the wilderness
And streams in the Arabah.
The scorched land will become a pool,
And the thirsty ground springs of water. (Isa. 35:1–7, NASB)

In the midst of the dryness of the desert, blossoms begin to appear out of nowhere. Beautiful flowers, of brilliant colour and exquisite in design, push their way up out of the dry earth. It is an awesome sight. This phenomenon is the same in our own lives – when we let go of our own means of coping, of trying to make things happen, and instead trust ourselves to the safety of Almighty God, even in the midst of the dryness of our lives, springs of living water bring forth blossom.

The world of the sheep is both negative – wilderness (emptiness, isolation, despair, danger) – and positive – blossom (promise, faith, provision). If you are in the *mid-bar* (wilderness) by yourself you can be in big trouble, but if you have a shepherd you are blessed. The shepherd is vital in leading, guiding, protecting and caring for the sheep. The sheep know the shepherd, listen to His voice and follow His command. Without the shepherd they are lost; with the shepherd the wilderness has potential. In biblical times the shepherds developed characteristics of leadership in the wilderness. In the same way we can find life in our wilderness; we can grow, we can mature, and we can become real.

"I suppose *you* are Real?" said the Rabbit. And then he wished he had not said it, for he thought the Skin Horse might be sensitive. But the Skin Horse only smiled.

"The Boy's Uncle made me Real," he said. "That was a great many years ago; but once you are Real you can't become unreal again. It lasts for always."[2]

## Notes

1. Marjory Williams, *The Velveteen Rabbit*, Miniature Edition (London: Egmont Books Ltd, 1993), p.5.
2. Ibid., p.8.
   Used with permission

# CHAPTER ELEVEN

# A KEY TO MANY

Emmy Wilson.

# Biography

Emmy Wilson spent 14 years training and practising as both a state registered nurse and a registered sick children's nurse, culminating in three years nursing those affected by HIV and AIDS. Emmy ended her nursing career when the Lord dramatically changed her heart, prompting her to take the Gospel to those in society whose lifestyles made them most vulnerable to this disease. This resulted in her joining the staff of Holy Trinity Brompton, London, in 1985 to begin the work of "The Earl's Court Project" (a Christian ministry responding to AIDS, prostitution, drug addiction and homelessness).

Emmy became involved in Prison work in 1991, helping as a part-time volunteer in the chaplaincy team at HMP Holloway. In late 1994 she began taking teams to other prisons in the UK to support chaplains who wanted to start using the Alpha course.

This work grew rapidly and an *Alpha* in Prisons department was created at HTB in July 1997. There are now four full time members of staff who work alongside Emmy to fulfil their twofold vision: to give every inmate in the UK the opportunity to attend an *Alpha* course and to help link every man or woman upon release with a church community that can support them.

Emmy has spoken about her work in Germany, Austria, Switzerland, Australia, New Zealand, Singapore, Hong Kong, Russia, Ireland, Canada and the USA.

In his heart a man plans his course,
but the Lord determines his steps (Prov. 16:9).

"Lord, I'm not called to prison ministry!" I repeated over and over again in my prayer times with my prayer partner. "I don't understand why I keep receiving invitations from chaplains to take a team to their prison. I'm not suited to this sort of work ..." But the invitations kept on coming. To be honest, ministering inside a prison was the furthest prospect from my mind.

Compassion for the broken-hearted and those imprisoned was not something I had always experienced. The Lord began the process of changing my heart and attitude towards people with completely different backgrounds to my own while I was nursing people with HIV and AIDS in the early 1980s. The Holy Spirit revealed to me that I was very judgemental and unloving. Reading from James 2:1–17, I was particularly impacted by verse 13: "Judgment without mercy will be shown to anyone who has not been merciful. Mercy triumphs over judgment!" With a privileged background and upbringing, how could I ever be accepted by those I seemed to be being called to work with? Why would they want to talk to me, let alone listen to what I might have to say?

My involvement with prisons began in 1990 when Sandy Millar, my vicar at Holy Trinity Brompton (HTB), first made me aware that he was on the Board of Visitors at Holloway Prison.

"What's the Board of Visitors?" I enquired.

"It's an independent watchdog, appointed by the Home Secretary, that visits on a regular basis, and listens to inmates or staff, and any issues they might have."

"Oh" was about all that I could say in response.

Sandy continued, "I was talking to the chaplain yesterday, and he was telling me how overworked he was. He asked me if I could recommend anyone from HTB who might be able to get involved with the pastoral needs of the women."

As I was on the pastoral staff at the church, I assumed that Sandy was asking for my advice, so that together we could think of someone in the congregation who would be suitable for the role. What he said next completely shocked me.

"Well, Em, I thought of you!"

"Oh no, Sandy, not prison ministry," I replied. The Earl's Court Project (which I had founded some five years before, offering help to people living in addictive lifestyles) had been a big enough surprise for me when the Lord called me out of my nursing career to begin a street work of outreach.

"Why are you asking me?" I asked nervously, not really wanting to hear the reason he might give!

"I just thought you would be rather good at it," was his brief response.

"Can I think and pray about this?" I enquired, and then we parted.

I trusted Sandy's judgement completely but I went home that evening thoroughly confused and, to be honest, in a state of bewilderment. Then I remembered a prophetic word I had received several months earlier. We had held a conference at HTB and invited John Wimber and a team from Kansas City to speak and teach about prophecy. I received a word, which I had been unable to comprehend or make sense of at the time.

"This sister's going to be right in the middle of the Salvation

Army – her calling is evangelism – and a teaching ministry to reveal Christ mightily, relieving the hood of sickness, sin and poverty. Instead of darkness they might have light. Instead of death they might have life. She will be a key to many, unchaining and unshackling those who cannot any longer free themselves."

"A key to many ..." I pondered these words, and had to admit that I could only relate keys with prisons. So, out of obedience to the Lord, ultimately, and to Sandy, I went back to Sandy with my response.

Within days I was being shown round and interviewed by the chaplain at Holloway Prison. I was utterly convinced that he would consider me totally unsuited to pastoral work with prisoners. I answered his questions carefully and, to my surprise, bordering on unbelief, he said at the end, "I would like you to start as soon as possible, but you do have to complete some application forms for the Home Office to check you out." I reckoned that would delay any decision by at least two or three weeks! So I filled them in and, in no particular hurry, posted them.

Weeks went by, and I heard nothing. "Phew", I thought, "something from my past must have caused the authorities to consider me unsuitable!"

I wondered if I should enquire of the chaplain, but decided I should lie low until he chose to contact me since I still had absolutely no desire to work in prison.

Several months passed, and still nothing. Then my father had a serious car crash, followed several months later by one of my sisters going through a difficult divorce. Then my father, still in his recovery, had a major nervous breakdown. I was torn between my family members, travelling back and forth visiting, comforting, encouraging and praying. I was torn emotionally between them and was often exhausted by the various needs and demands. I almost forgot I had ever been inside Holloway Prison.

The following summer I travelled to a Greek island, Skiathos, with some friends on holiday. On the flight, I met a couple who I didn't know very well. While waiting for our luggage to appear at Skiathos Airport, the wife pulled out a book from her hand luggage, and said, "I think you should read this while you're on holiday."

What she didn't know was that I am a very slow reader and I already had my two holiday books in my luggage. I certainly did *not* want a third book to read! But I graciously took the book, and started it the next morning. It was called *Rescued by Love* by Jenny Davies – and described how she had shot her husband dead after discovering he was having a homosexual affair. The night before she went into Holloway Prison her young daughter prostrated herself across her mother's bed crying, "Mummy, you can't leave me and go into prison!"

On the day she was admitted, she had a vision of Jesus in her cell and, as a result, her entire sentence was totally transformed.

I wept my way through this heartbreaking account in a mere 24 hours, then handed the book back. To my surprise, Rachael announced that she had another book she thought I should read. What was so strange was that I had never discussed with her about my interview at Holloway some 11 months previously. By now my attention had been grasped, and I read the second book just as quickly. It was called *The Pastor's Wife* by Sabina Wurmbrand. I knew her husband, Richard, had been in prison at the end of the Second World War because of his faith, but I had no idea that Sabina had been as well. It was her account of sharing a cell with 50 other inmates – one slop-out bucket and filthy conditions; stomachs swollen with hunger and rampant disease. As I lay on the beach – with the sun shining, the sea lapping at my feet, the birds soaring in clear blue skies – I remember thinking to myself, "Who am I to say I can't bring some of Your love, Your life, and Your 'freedom' into prison, Lord?"

Within ten days of my holiday ending, I received a phone call from the chaplain at Holloway saying, "I'm so sorry, your papers were passed months ago by the Home Office, but I've only just discovered them under a large pile on my desk. When can you start here?"

To my surprise, I heard myself reply, "As soon as you would like me to."

So out of pure obedience to the Lord, I began to visit Holloway Prison. I felt like a fish out of water. I loathed the shouting and swearing, the sound of doors banging shut ahead of me and behind me. I have always been mildly claustrophobic, and to be locked through every door until we arrived at the chaplain's department made me want to "escape" as soon as I could.

On my first visit, the chaplain brought two sisters to see me in the department. I have to admit, I hardly understood a word they said to me. They had such broad East London accents and the prison terminology was so new to me that I found it extremely hard to follow them. Drawing a very deep breath at the end of my hour, I asked if I could pray with them. I felt that if I didn't start that day as I meant to continue, I might never venture back the following week. To my surprise, they accepted my offer, even though they were not Christians. As they left, I felt exhausted by the whole experience, and wondered how I would ever get used to this ministry. I felt completely out of my depth.

However, I persevered. To my total surprise, the second week the chaplain gave me keys, and sent me off on my own to the wings to visit someone, and then said it was up to me as to who else I should visit. I felt as if I was thrown in to the lions' den. As I walked through the wings, girls would shout at me, "Are you Probation, Miss?"

"No", I replied, "I'm from the Chaplaincy" (hoping that might inspire them to ask if they could chat to me).

Gradually, I started to get to know some of the women, and then they would ask me to return the following week to see them again.

The Lord used my three and a half years at Holloway Prison as a training ground. As I helped the chaplain with the various pastoral needs he had to contend with daily, I learnt from the women themselves the sad and painful truths as to why they had ended up behind bars. Many had grown up in children's homes. I heard accounts of abuse – physical, spiritual, emotional or sexual. Parents who were divorced, separated or absent themselves – some serving prison sentences like their children. Latchkey kids, bored at the end of the day, experimenting with alcohol, smoking, and all too soon, drugs of various kinds. Women from Nigeria, Uganda, Zambia, Kenya, Barbados, Jamaica, Peru, Colombia, caught on their way through Heathrow smuggling drugs, and now serving long sentences, leaving ageing mothers or other relatives back home to bring up five, six, seven or more children. I sat for hours talking, listening and praying with them, and sharing my own life too. Every week, as the final gate banged shut behind me I would say to the Lord, "There, but for the grace of God, go I ..."

Why was I so fortunate to grow up in a loving family, with

parents who showed me nothing but generous and continuous love? I never heard them quarrel, shout at each other, fight or get angry. I always felt safe and secure. What a terrible contrast to the tragic life histories that were retold to me week by week.

There was one lady, Mabel, whom I regularly visited and prayed with. One week, when I went to see her, she was lying in bed in great pain. She had hurt her back, and was unable to care for her baby as she had been bedbound all over the weekend. The officers and other mums on the mother and baby unit had helped look after them. Despite her pain, Mabel could tell that I was particularly excited about something, and soon I was unfolding the events of the previous fortnight.

It was 1994, and I had been overwhelmed by Jesus' love as the Holy Spirit filled me over and over again. I had fallen in love with Jesus in a completely new way. All fear of people had left me. My heart thumped, my knees felt weak, I laughed, I wept for all I knew who had yet to profess faith in Jesus. I cried out to God to touch even the hardest hearts through His Holy Spirit so that they might experience the extraordinary power that was transforming my own relationship with Jesus. "Lord, I'm totally abandoned to You – I don't mind where You send me – I just love You with all my heart!" The freedom and exhilaration that came with relinquishing everything to the Lord was amazing.

I had once heard Keith Green (a worship leader tragically killed in an aeroplane accident) say that he was "bananas for Jesus". I remember thinking at the time, that I doubted I would ever be heard saying the same myself. Yet, overnight I had become exactly that and Mabel could see the transformation. I spent some time telling her how the Holy Spirit was moving powerfully around the world, and then I offered to pray for her back. She slowly and carefully struggled to sit up and perch on the edge of her bed. As I prayed, the pain seemingly worsened.

After a while, I needed to move on to visit some of the other women. As I left her cell, she asked me if I would tell the other mums, who had gathered to feed their babies at tea time, how the Holy Spirit was moving in a new way around the world.

"Do you really want me to?" I responded.

And so I found myself, watched by ten mums and their babies, with my arms opened wide, exclaiming: "Listen everyone! The Holy Spirit is moving powerfully around the world ..."

Suddenly, Mabel appeared from her cell behind me, and started leaping up and down in the air, shouting, "My back is healed! My back is healed!"

All the women pointed at her in total astonishment saying, "That has to be God! We know you couldn't get out of bed all weekend. That has to be God!"

Then each mum asked me to pray for her. I was amazed, as normally it took several visits before I knew someone well enough for it to seem right to suggest that we prayed together.

There was one more remarkable incident! When I asked one lady what she would like me to pray for, she told me she was being deported the following day to Nairobi, but please could I pray that she went to New York instead. "Why do you want to go to New York?" I asked.

"Because my other children and my husband live there," was her response.

"Fair enough," I thought! If I was her, I would want to be reunited with my husband and other children too.

I remember praying: "Lord, I'm not sure how You will manage this, but please help Helen to go to New York tomorrow, not Nairobi ... Amen."

I finished praying with all the other mums, and then went on to visit some other women.

The following Monday, Mabel was in terrific form. Her back was fine! During the course of my visit, I enquired if she had ever heard from Helen after her deportation. "Oh yes," she replied. "She rang last Wednesday."

"Where was she ringing from?" I asked.

"From New York," came the astonishing reply!

Helen had been just about to board the aircraft, when an official suddenly appeared, told her she was on the wrong flight and should follow him. They walked back up through the departure gate, along the corridors, and finally to another gate, where the plane's destination was ... New York!

Recently, while speaking on the *Alpha* Holy Spirit day at Send Prison, I recounted this story during the course of the day. One inmate excitedly put up her hand and said, "That story is true! I knew Helen, and she *did* go to New York, not Nairobi." What an awesome, incredible God!

Six months after Mabel's back was healed, as I stood in Exeter Prison's chapel, surrounded by 30 to 40 inmates, on my first visit inside a men's prison, I smiled inwardly as I remembered what I had declared to the Lord in my new-found love and abandonment. The wonderful and extraordinary reality was that I did not feel remotely frightened or apprehensive about being there. I was quietly confident that if He had called me to work in prisons, then He would equip me in the place He had called me to.

I was leading a team of seven people from HTB at the invitation of Bill Birdwood, Head Chaplain. Bill had been approached by one of the inmates, Michael, whose girlfriend was on the *Alpha* course at HTB. After only a few weeks, she had been so enthusiastic about *Alpha* that she had visited

Michael and said he must do the course too. He asked Bill who, in turn, contacted HTB to invite Nicky Gumbel to go down and tell them about the course. Nicky was keen to go but was constrained by his busy diary. He told Bill that although he couldn't go, he knew someone he could send. The following morning, I received a phone call from Nicky.

"Em, you do prison work," he said. "Please ring Bill Birdwood at Exeter Prison and arrange to take a team down."

"I couldn't possibly do that, Nicky!" was my instant response. "I've only ever worked in Holloway – a women's prison. I could never go into a male prison like Exeter!"

"Just speak to the chaplain," replied Nicky reassuringly. "He sounds really nice."

So I did, and he was! Before I knew it, my diary was open and a date was written in – 14 December 1994.

I had no conception that this visit to Exeter Prison was the beginning of an entirely new ministry at HTB. As invitations became more prolific from prison chaplains to help launch the *Alpha* course in their prison, I knew, above everything, that I needed to: "Trust in the Lord with all your heart and lean not on your own understanding; in all your ways acknowledge him, and he will make your paths straight" (Prov. 3:5–6).

Today, with *Alpha* running in over 80 per cent of the UK's prisons, I know I am called to:

preach good news to the poor. He has sent me to bind up the broken-hearted, to proclaim freedom for the captives and release from darkness for the prisoners, to proclaim the year of the Lord's favour and the day of vengeance of our God, to comfort all who mourn, and provide for those who grieve in Zion – to bestow on them a crown of beauty instead of ashes, the oil of gladness instead of mourning ...

They will be called oaks of righteousness, a planting of the Lord for the display of his splendour. (Isa. 61:1–4)

I am so grateful to the Lord that "He determines our steps".

# Encouraging Women

Contributors: Irene Addison, Anne Atkins, Jeannette Barwick, Fiona Castle, Margaret Ellis, Michele Guinness, Liz Hansford, Reona Joly, Liz Trundle, Jennifer Rees Larcombe, Priscilla Reid and Elaine Storkey.

*Encouraging Women* is packed with thoughtful and challenging teaching, with testimonies by respected Christian women. Great writing combines with refreshing candour to make this book essential reading for today's Christian woman. A wonderful gift for all ages.

ISBN: 1-85345-135-5
£6.99 (plus P&P)

Irene Addison
Anne Atkins
Jeannette Barwick
Fiona Castle
Margaret Ellis
Michele Guinness
Liz Hansford
Reona Joly
Liz Trundle
Jennifer Rees Larcombe
Priscilla Reid
Elaine Storkey

ENCOURAGING
*Women*

*Christian women write on living out their faith*

# God is Good for Women

There have always been women who have challenged the system and forced change. In this fascinating and inspiring book Michele Guinness talks about those who have broken new ground in very different ways.

We meet a range of professions, including a rabbi, a police superintendent, an army lieutenant colonel, a chief executive and a gynaecologist. All have extraordinary insights about what it is to be a woman in a relationship with God.

ISBN: 1-85345-263-7

£6.99 (plus P&P)

MICHELE GUINNESS

God is
Good for
Women

*Stories of notable women of faith*

*Alive for God* was a series of faith-building events drawing women together for celebration and encouragement.

*Woman Alive* magazine and CWR (Crusade for World Revival) launched *Alive for God* in 1998 in response to a need amongst Christian women to worship and to learn together. Combining lively worship with practical teaching, it endeavoured to focus on women as women before God, rather than the roles they might fulfil.

All writers in *Inspiring Women* have spoken at some stage at *Alive for God.*

*Alive for God* visited Bristol, Bournemouth, Belfast, Southampton, Bracknell, Birmingham, Glasgow, Sheffield, Brighton, Leicester and Manchester.

*Woman Alive* is the only UK magazine specifically written for today's Christian woman. Month by month, *Woman Alive* provides:

- A feast of fresh ideas, insight and encouragement
- Real life experiences and testimonies
- Spiritual topics to build your faith
- Practical advice, life skills and laughter
- Personality interviews
- Top Christian writers and columnists every month
- Contemporary issues discussed from a biblical perspective
- Faith in the workplace – at home and at work

"*Woman Alive* is ideal – challenging, informing, comforting and relaxing" – Catherine, Worcester.

*Woman Alive* can also be invaluable in your church women's group for discussion topics, teaching, discipleship and fuel for prayer. The contributors to this book also write for *Woman Alive*, so to read more ...

Subscribe to *Woman Alive* by phoning 01903 602136

Find out more about our ACTIV8 church resource pack, which includes *Woman Alive* magazine.

Write to:     Woman Alive
              Garcia Estate
              Canterbury Road
              Worthing
              West Sussex BN13 1EH

# Trusted
## All Over the World

**Daily Devotionals**

**Books and Videos**

**Day and Residential Courses**

**Counselling Training**

**Biblical Study Courses**

**Regional Seminars**

**Ministry to Women**

CWR have been providing training and resources for Christians since the 1960s. From our headquarters at Waverley Abbey House we have been serving God's people with a vision to help apply God's Word to everyday life and relationships. The daily devotional *Every Day with Jesus* is read by over three-quarters of a million people in more than 150 countries, and our unique courses in biblical studies and pastoral care are respected all over the world.

CWR  CRUSADE FOR WORLD REVIVAL  *Applying God's Word to everyday life and relationships*